6 95

# The SINGLE HEART

# *The* SINGLE HEART

Melinda Jennings

*Bookcraft*
Salt Lake City, Utah

Library of Congress Catalog Card Number: 84-70436
ISBN 0-88494-525-1

First Printing, 1984

Lithographed in the United States of America
PUBLISHERS PRESS
Salt Lake City, Utah

*To Amy*

*who has been an inspiration*

*in writing and in life*

# 1

Carolyn Jackson fell into the couch, a comb of fingers pulling back the twists of rich, dark hair that had strayed onto her pretty face. "Sorry I'm late."

"That's okay. Do you want to stay after for thirty minutes, or write fifty times 'I will never be late to presidency meeting'?" asked Rose.

Normally Carolyn would have laughed, but this morning she responded with a weak smile.

After the opening prayer, Rose Adams shifted her bulky weight before reading last week's minutes and then consulted notes similar to those of any ward Relief Society president. But her ward was different. Her sisters were different. They were single.

She stared up from the scribbles. Her counselors resembled each other enough to be sisters. If Rose looked like either of them, she would be married by now. "Carolyn, you're planning a teacher's workshop, aren't you? Can you bring us up to date on that?"

Carolyn, always efficient, flipped open to the yellow tab in her notebook. "Oh, no." She was looking at a sheet entitled "Teachers' Workshop." It should have been entitled "rainbow cyclone," because it was covered with the crayon artwork of a toddler. Her fingers turned quickly through the other pages, many just as colorful. "Those kids!"

Suzann, sitting next to Carolyn, leaned over in search of an explanation. Suzann gave hers. "Someone thought they found a coloring book."

"My sister's kids," supplied Carolyn. "Alice had a baby three days ago, and at home we've been watching Tyler, who's four, Janice, who's three, and Josh, who's twenty months— watching them tear up the house."

"When you're not used to having children around, they can disrupt everything," said Rose.

"And sometimes when you're used to having them around." Suzann, who had been Mrs. White, was still the mother of two. When her marriage had ended, her steward-ship over the children had increased.

Carolyn was thinking revenge, like cutting a birthday budget in half. She turned to Suzann. "How do you manage to keep anything intact?"

"Our place is held together by Scotch tape. Actually, at three and seven my children are growing out of the destructive stage. They save their energy for bickering."

Carolyn shook her head. "I think I can make out the work-shop plans, Rose. Do you still want to hear about it?"

"Yes. And make it colorful."

The outline sounded fine. "What's next?" Rose returned to her notes. "We're in charge of food for the lake trip. It won't be for over a month, but we should be thinking about a menu and getting assignments made."

*Hot dogs, Oreos—who cares what we have,* thought Caro-lyn. She was trying to unfrazzle her mind. Friday the kids had blasted into the home she shared with her parents, throwing everything off balance. The house used to seem large, but for the past few days there hadn't been a crevice that could insure privacy. It used to seem neat, but lately it had been impos-sible to walk into the kitchen without stepping on a Lego, or running into a drawer that had been left open, or smashing the remains of a peanut butter and jelly sandwich into the floor. It used to be quiet, but now when there wasn't squealing or shouting there were cries for crackers and juice—and the questions. Out of every ten sentences Tyler spoke, nine were questions. "Why do you keep your shampoo there?" "What did you put the shortening in for?" "How does this work? No, not how do you turn it on, what makes it work inside?"

It wasn't that Carolyn didn't love the children. They were stars, each of them, with shining faces and twinkling eyes—especially if she gave them a little attention. But they never quite stayed in the distance. They were right there, into everything. They had dumped the transparencies out of a slide carousel and were constantly stripping the cushions off the couches to make forts. Carolyn could live with those kinds of inconveniences; what strained her tolerance was discovering that they had decorated the bathroom walls with her makeup. Then, this morning while she'd been eating breakfast, Janice had cut a paper doll out of a homework assignment her professor would be expecting tomorrow.

At least Carolyn didn't have sole responsibility for the children. Her mother, and her father when he was home, were also kept hopping. And there were reposes. She had spent part of the day in classes Friday, and last night she had been out with Jesse. And how could she think about anything else when she was with Jesse?

When had she known he was different? When had she started holding her breath for his smiles? When had he become the star of her dreams?

It hadn't been this way in the beginning. She couldn't even pinpoint where she had first noticed him. At a dance? Sitting in church? She was certain he'd been at the Hawaiian dinner. But before she had ever recognized his face, she had known enough about him to write a story. All of her friends were talking about Jesse. "Jesse has a face you could stare at for three weeks." "Jesse made five straight baskets in the fourth quarter and won the game for our team." "Have you heard Jesse play the piano?" But that couldn't be enough—to be dashing and talented. No. Jesse had to add the finishing touch that made him the most eligible bachelor in the Forty-ninth Ward —the singles ward. At twenty-six he had his own successful business. Or businesses; he did a handful of things. Like write software programs for computers. No one knew exactly how much he was worth, but the estimates started at half a million dollars.

Carolyn had just laughed at the enthusiasm of her friends. "Do me a favor and try to resist proposing, okay?" And she told herself she wasn't going to be impressed.

When she finally caught sight of their hero, she couldn't say he didn't have a nice face—arresting, dark eyes and a straight nose. His thick brown hair waved in just the right places and his tall, lean body needed no alterations. But he wasn't the ultimate in looks. Now that her curiosity had been satisfied, she could get along without him. In fact, she rarely saw Jesse. Not until the women's softball team started their season did she have any real interaction with him. He was the coach.

He spoke his first words to her at practice. "Carolyn, you're holding the bat wrong."

She looked up at him from over the plate. "I'm not holding it wrong. I'm holding it different."

"Okay. You're holding it different. Do you want to know how to hold it right?"

"If I don't get two good hits in the first game, you can change my swing."

And then he had smiled at her. Dimples. And such nice, straight teeth. The smile had struck her like a secret weapon. She had been so determined not to join his throng of admirers, and then he had flashed that smile to make her question her decision. Well, it wouldn't work.

So it wasn't the alluring smile that changed her opinion; it was the way Jesse coached the team. He offered valuable tips and suggestions. When a team member pulled in a nice catch or whacked a solid hit, he shouted, waving a clenched fist, and always acknowledged the feat once more when she returned to the bench. Sometimes he teased them; for example, if one of them let a ball get by in practice he'd yell, "Six times around the field." And when Leslie had stalled between third and home to be tagged out, Jesse had said, "You can't stop, Leslie. Even if you had an engagement ring and it fell in the dirt, you'd keep running if you were ahead of the ball like that." But when someone made a humiliating error and wanted to crawl under one of the base bags, Jesse never taunted. He just said, "Don't worry about it" or "You'll get it next time."

4

It was during the softball season that Carolyn decided it might be nice to go out with Jesse. He never asked her, though. He dated and she dated, but not each other. And when finally they did connect for lunch, it was Carolyn's doing, not Jesse's.

Two weeks after the team had taken second in the playoffs, after Jesse had shed the role of coach, Carolyn discovered in an English class that he could be useful to her again. The instructor had just challenged the class members to write a paper on something that was rocking the world, but which they knew very little about. Carolyn thought of computers, and she thought of Jesse.

She made an appointment to see him. Jesse rented office space in a new Spanish-style building that made a square around a garden with a beautifully tiled fountain. Carolyn approached a door marked with gold letters, "Jesse Mitchell— Data Software and Systems." The waiting room bespoke the services of a professional decorator. Compelling pencil drawings and watercolors arrested the eye like museum pieces, and plants that bubbled over unusual ceramic containers added the breath of life. Carolyn gave her name to a secretary old enough to be Jesse's mother, then looked more closely at the artwork as she waited, rather than sinking into the upholstered cloud of a couch or one of the matching chairs.

Jesse came out to greet her. "Hello, Carolyn. Come in." And they walked back to his office.

"This is nice, Jesse—but have you ever lost anyone in that couch?"

Jesse smiled. He wasn't sitting behind the big oak desk cluttered with books and papers; instead they sat in facing chairs. "Not yet, but if I did, I'm sure they'd let me return it."

"You really have a nice place."

"Thanks. I enjoy what I'm doing. That's the important thing."

Oh, yes. I agree."

"But I'm surprised to see you. What can I help you with?"

"I'm doing some research for a paper," she told him. "I'd like to find out how computers have changed in the past five years."

Jesse's eyes left her face for a few moments while he delved into his memory and then they returned.

"Computers are sassier," he answered. "I was working with a program the other day and decided to erase some material. I enacted the command and the computer asked, "Are you sure you want to delete?' I typed *Yes.* Instead of instant compliance, the computer held back. 'Then type *Please.*' "

Carolyn grinned.

"Now," continued Jesse, "I'll give you something you can use."

"I can use that. It's the kind of introduction I was looking for."

Then Jesse plunged into talk about compatibility and megabytes and disk density while Carolyn asked questions and took notes. She had several pages of scribbles when he stopped and studied her.

"Is that pen your lunch?" he asked.

She hadn't realized she was chewing on it. "No. I had one for breakfast."

He smiled. "Are you hungry? Let's go eat." And in Jesse's 280ZX they darted to a Mexican restaurant down the street.

"Well, Carolyn, I never got to correct the way you bat," Jesse told her when they were seated under a painting of a matador snapping his fiery cape. "You're not a bad softball player."

"My dad taught me. Drilled me, even. You'd think I was a boy. But I was his last child, his third daughter. I think he pretended I was a boy."

"He doesn't still?"

"Not as much. When I turned nineteen and didn't go on a mission, he stopped buying me athletic equipment for my birthday."

Jesse chuckled. They didn't notice at first that the waitress was standing by to take their order. Carolyn asked for some flautas and Jesse decided on the enchilada dinner.

"Are you from Mesa, Jesse? I don't know anything about you." Instantly Carolyn remembered all the statistics dumped on her by friends, and she laughed. It came out just as Jesse answered, "Tempe."

"No, Carolyn. I wasn't being funny."

"I know. I'm sorry. Tempe, huh? That's wonderful."

But he was just looking at her.

"I can tell you expect me to explain why I laughed."

"If you don't, I'll have a complex for the rest of my life about the place I was raised."

She didn't want to explain. *Think fast.* "Haven't you heard what they say about people from Tempe? Supposedly they do the strangest things, like peel the candy shells off M and M's before they eat them and drive on the left side of the road after midnight and try to change everybody's softball swing."

"That's not it at all," Jesse had laughed. "They only peel the shells off yellow and orange M and M's, and they just drive on the left side of the road after midnight on odd numbered days, and if someone gets two good hits in the first game, they leave her swing alone."

And Carolyn laughed, too. Their food, piled on sizzling-hot plates that threatened to brand the table, was being set in front of them. She had escaped telling Jesse he was all her friends could talk about.

Lunch was over too fast. Carolyn ordered ice cream just to stretch out the meal, but she couldn't really dawdle or she'd have been sucking her dessert through a straw. Jesse had seemed interested in her, and she had captivated enough young men to know when one was on the hook, but he didn't mention future plans when he let her out next to her car.

If Jesse wasn't scheming to get them together, fate was. That Sunday night they both walked into the church foyer while the opening prayer of a fireside was in progress. They found chairs together in the back of the chapel. When the program ended, Carolyn was able to accept his offer of a ride home because she had been left at the building by her parents. She invited him inside, and they sat separated by a flower in the fabric of her living room couch.

Jesse had studied her leisurely. "So . . . the legend."

"What?"

As he shook his head, she figured out he might have been talking about her.

"Wait a minute," said Carolyn. "I think you're a little mixed up. *I'm* not the computer whiz kid. What have I done that makes me a legend?"

Jesse just looked at her, as though he were deciding whether to believe her or not. And then, unexpectedly, he kissed her. Not just a peck, a real kiss. A kiss of such finesse it made Carolyn wonder if he had been perfecting the kiss instead of computer programs all these years.

Then he drew back. "What have I done? I wasn't even going to take you out, and here I am kissing you."

Carolyn pulled back, too. "I didn't know my reputation was that bad."

"Oh I've heard terrible things about you. That you're clever and dynamic, even entrancing. But I've heard that you play games. I'm twenty-six and tired of playing games."

"I don't play games. I'm just not in the market for a husband."

"Don't tell me I've found the needle in the haystack—the only girl in the Forty-ninth Ward who doesn't have her wedding dress picked out."

"Come on. I know at least one other girl who hasn't decided on the color her bridesmaids will be wearing."

"I won't hold my breath to find her."

"I know several."

"You can't name one," he challenged.

"Suzann White. She gets opportunities to date, but isn't interested."

"But she's already been married. She's probably had a bad experience."

"Sorry, Jesse, it's too late to make qualifications. I've already won the jackpot, taken it home, and spent it."

He narrowed his eyes until for a moment he was looking at her through slits. "You are clever, Carolyn. You just might be everything they say about you."

"You'll have to find out for yourself."

"I know. I was just wondering if I should do that."

Carolyn had to say something light; she was losing control of the conversation. "Why don't we draw straws?"

Jesse smiled. "See, you have me playing your games already."

That was when they started dating each other. Regularly and exclusively, right from the beginning. But now Carolyn was afraid she wasn't playing games any more. She was getting serious. Too serious for a girl who wasn't in the market for a husband. And she would have to tell Jesse that they couldn't see each other as much, that they should start dating other people. No. She could never say that to Jesse. But a weekend with Alice's children confirmed her feeling that she wasn't ready for marriage and a family. She'd have to tell him.

# 2

"Carolyn. Carolyn?" It was Rose. Her voice flowed into a soothing song. "When I count to three and snap my fingers you will awaken, remembering everything that has happened."

Carolyn smiled. Rose. She loved Rose. "That's okay. I'm conscious now."

"We've been going over the names for the new women's directory—adding, scratching, changing. Do you know of any alterations that need to be made?"

"Ummm, Sandy Eckol's cousin has moved down from Snowflake and is staying with her now."

"We've got that one."

"Did you change Jenny Brimhall's phone number? The last two numbers are reversed on the current list."

"We've switched those, too."

"Well, I'm going back into my trance, then."

"No, wait." Rose reached out a hand as if she were going to shake her. "Did you check with Jesse about letting us type our list on his computer?"

"Oh, I did," interrupted Suzann. "He's my home teacher and I asked him when he and Paul visited last week. He said it would be fine. He'd be glad to show someone how to do it."

"Good." Rose marked on her pad. "Tina Johnson has offered to be our typist."

*Tina? She's been stalking Jesse for months,* thought Carolyn. *She's only looking for a chance to move in on him.* She shook her head. *Wait. I can't keep thinking about Jesse as mine.*

"Well, that's it, girls." Rose leaned back and smiled at them. "The Relief Society has been wound up for another week."

"Is Elaine feeling better?" asked Suzann, referring to their secretary, down with a virus.

"A little. Oh, I made some cinnamon rolls last night and promised to send her some. Can you drop them by?"

"I could, but I didn't have breakfast and I'm not sure all the rolls would make it," answered Suzann.

Rose was up and into the kitchen. "Would I send you and Carolyn away without one for the road?"

The rolls were big—twice as high as the ones that come wrapped in cellophane. And they were lighter, Rose said, because she added two cups of air. They were impossible to eat without getting icing all over everything. If one indulged while driving a car, as Suzann did on her way to Elaine's, the icing spread to the steering wheel and gearshift as well.

At Elaine's apartment, Suzann set the bag of rolls on the doormat, punched the bell, and retreated beyond the porch.

"I'm not playing ring and run. I'm taking precautions," she called, when Elaine appeared at the door in a robe. "I can't get the flu until my kids grow up."

Elaine nodded and waved.

Being sick and a single parent should be two conditions that preclude each other, thought Suzann. Two of the darkest days in her life had accompanied the flu six weeks after she had been left alone with the children. Not six weeks and twenty-four hours, just six weeks. During the first year of her independence Suzann had scratched off the days on the wall of her heart; she'd known exactly when the 103-degree fever had forced her to bed. Kevin, sixteen months old then, had showed his sympathy by using her as a jungle gym, his slightest pressure intensifying the pain; Suzann had turned away and wept. Trisha, who'd been five, had made a real effort to be helpful. She hadn't meant for the toast to catch fire or for the orange juice to spill or for Kevin to grab the eggs when she opened the refrigerator.

As a married mother, Suzann had thought there was nothing worse than being sick with small children. Now she knew that being alone and sick with small children was worse.

Suzann's Chevette glided into the carport, bumping into the parking block stenciled with chipping, black letters: "White." She walked through the rasping wooden gate of their tiny backyard, scattered with more than a few children's toys, and entered the lower level of their condominium. Even during the day Suzann couldn't walk into her empty home without wondering if a would-be-assailant was awaiting her. Insecurity. Another aspect of being alone. And daylight fears were gentle compared to the terrors that invaded her nights.

The agony was not in the moments between the pillow and sleep—they were so few. Rather, it came when she had embraced with such dependency the soothing, rejuvenating balm of slumber. Then that slumber turned against her. Not suddenly, but like a piano piece that builds from an airy melody to heavy, violent chords. Oftentimes she started out with an ordinary dream, but gradually she recognized the notes foreshadowing an inevitable evil. But how could that be? Everything was fine, normal. No. She was in danger. And her child was in danger. Just one child? A baby. Was it Trisha or Kevin that she carried wrapped in a ragged blanket? They walked through the neighborhood of Suzann's childhood. She knew it, although it was dark, devoid of the glow from even one porch light. And she knew they were being followed. Run! Run home! She was trying. Her legs were leaden. The coat of the black silhouette behind them was flapping. Run! She was approaching her home, her haven. She was on the porch, fumbling with the handle. Somebody open the door! Open the door! Somebody, *open the door!* Open your eyes.

And Suzann would awaken, as always, before the crucial moment. The clock and her heart beat a rhythm together in the night and for some time the terror and urgency of the dream remained more convincing than the shadows of her bedroom.

Eventually the menacing night would fade into the pressures of the day. Seventeen waking hours weren't enough, twenty weren't, for all Suzann needed to do. On weekdays, Kevin, Trisha, and Suzann dressed and said a family prayer. Then the kids ate breakfast from a box and they were off. Suzann paid a close friend to take care of her children while Jarvis, Brown, and Jenson paid Suzann to take care of the phone, type letters, and prepare legal papers. That was the easy part. At five she was threading through traffic to Trisha and Kevin and the rest of her responsibilities. In the evenings she made dinner and cleared dinner and consulted the schedule to see if it was time to mop or vacuum or scour bathrooms or dust or wash or get groceries or have a nervous breakdown. She tried to halt the list of duties that cycled through her mind long enough to listen when her children wanted to tell or ask her something, but sometimes the button was jammed. Even though she saw their faces and noticed that their mouths were moving, she could only think about what she'd have to rearrange before vacuuming and whether or not she had the necessary ingredients to throw a casserole together and that she needed to write "detergent" on the shopping list. That was the part that made her want to scream. She longed to give her children a feast of love and attention, but she could only offer them a crumb.

At least they had weekends. Well, every other weekend. It took the whole preceding week to plan for a Saturday they would spend together. And whether they chose a picnic in the park or rollerskating or making a special craft, the concluding activity remained constant. They always ended with a hot fudge sundae at Mary Coyle's ice cream parlor.

So Saturdays gave Suzann a crack at that devoted mother ideal which was so transient during the week. But sometimes she felt not like a parent but a playmate, a fellow Columbus in a strange, new world. Often it was those days that they would find themselves snatching pieces of months later, attached to a "remember when." And occasionally there was a day everyone wanted to forget.

Almost a year ago they had arranged to see Walt Disney's *Lady and the Tramp*, but under the conditions that Kevin would pick up his Loc Blocs and Trisha would have some peanut-butter-and-honey sandwiches ready to eat on the way. Suzann had reminded them each three times, and they had heard her over the Saturday morning cartoons, but they just hadn't been mobilized into action. When they should have left for the theater, the Loc Blocs were clearly visible and the sandwiches were not. Suzann called off the outing, and the children whined. Kevin said if they didn't see the movie he would never pick up his Loc Blocs, but Suzann remained firm.

Trisha handled her disappointment by picking on Kevin. She told him the boy he had drawn looked like an ant, and that out of all the people she knew, he was the least like Spiderman. She baited him into a game of Candyland, but the cards had been stacked to send Trisha immediately to the ice cream floats and become one of the fastest winners in history.

Then Kevin, who was in the process of being toilet trained, had his third accident that day. Suzann was rinsing his training pants in the toilet while he stood by, defiantly glaring at her. It was too much. She was trying not to be upset, but she couldn't get the meter below furious. It had been so easy with Trisha. And that glare! She gave him a stinging swat across his fleshy bottom. There. He was howling. But the momentary release was overshadowed by the guilt of a mother who felt that toilet training should be a low-keyed affair; a mother who was sympathetic to the proponents of nonviolent child raising; a mother who lived in mortal fear of the words, "I love Daddy more." Besides that, the timing was bad; Suzann had released the underpants to strike just after she had flushed, and the pants had twisted down with the suction. Not down and away into the sewer—just down the pipes to plug up the toilet. A neighbor gave Suzann her first lesson on how to use a plunger, but no one gave her an ear to unclog the tangle of frustrations that had built up inside her.

But of all the things that were difficult about being single, one trial had the greatest capacity for inflicting pain. It wasn't the insecurity, the relentless burden, or the feeling obligated to forsake her favorite articles in a magazine to read "Ten Car Noises You Shouldn't Ignore." It wasn't explaining to someone that you were divorced and watching him try to figure out the flaw that made you unbearable to live with. The real agony was knowing Peter was with someone else.

Suzann could feel her memory load the tape. She had played the scene so many times she couldn't believe it wasn't worn out. But there she was—lying in Peter's arms, after an evening she had designed to be magic. Looking into his face, seeing the tears, she'd read it as a sign of her success—she'd thought they were tears of joy. But the tension in Peter's face had tipped her off.

"What's wrong, Peter? What's the matter?"

"Suzann, I'm so sorry."

Then she started to brace herself. Someone has died, she thought. Peter knows and has to tell me. She disciplined the mounting alarm into composure—breathe in, breathe out—and gazed intently into his face.

"I'm in love with someone else."

"What?" The word popped out even though she had heard him. "Wait. Don't say it again. It's not true."

"I'm so sorry, Suzann."

And she turned away from him, trying to stop the words, shut off the pain, not feel. But his voice penetrated her barrier.

"I didn't mean for it to happen. Marta and I were assigned to do some projects together. It was just business—sales programs—but gradually we started adding details about ourselves. She was having problems with her boyfriend and asked for advice. Then we were meeting in my office and talking for hours without even mentioning projected figures."

"Peter, stop. Maybe one day I'll want to hear all about it." A tear tickled her nose and she realized she was crying, too. "This might come as a surprise to you, but it isn't that comforting to learn how natural it was to fall in love with her."

And against her instinct, Suzann twisted to face him. Even tearstained, even contorted in pain, his face was handsome. She shouldn't have turned.

"I'm sorry," he said. Then he had reached for her, to comfort her, but she had intercepted his hands and placed them on her neck.

"If you really want to stop the pain, just squeeze, Peter. Squeeze and don't let go until I say 'stop.' "

15

He jerked his hands away and drew tight fists back to his body. "Suzann, I would take my own life before I'd take yours."

It was hard to know who had been in more agony that night, but Peter had left with his anguish while Suzann knew there was no place on earth she could go to escape hers. The only life preserver she could cling to was the conviction that he'd come back. He still loved her. And they would get married again. Only Peter would join the Church. Next time they'd get married in the temple.

# 3

Suzann blew out a deep breath and fingered a pen which had been lying on the end table. "Peter," she said softly, "why does your image intrude so persistently, while the you I could touch hesitates to return?"

She wondered if she was obligated to call Rose. Was her despondency acute enough? Maybe she would cheat this time and suffer alone.

They had made their pact several months ago, when Rose had come by unexpectedly to drop off some Relief Society material. It was on a Saturday, just twenty minutes after the kids had been picked up by Peter. And Marta. When Suzann answered the door with red eyes, Rose beheld her as if she were a motherless child.

"Suzann. What is it?" Rose led her to the couch and sat them both down.

"It's nothing. Just my life."

"I'm glad it's nothing." Rose looked steadily into her eyes. "Let me tell you about *my* problems. I'm still in love with the man I used to be married to. And sometimes I think about him. And us. And—worst of all—them. And it's hard and it hurts and no one cares."

Suzann smiled because Rose had never been married, yet she knew her friend so well.

Then Rose continued, "Now it's your turn again. I want to know every single thing that's wrong. I'm not moving until either I've heard it all or it's time to pick up my mom at the airport—but that's not for two weeks."

And after Suzann had emptied her heart, she found that it no longer lay heavy as a boulder in her chest.

"I'm better, Rose. Thanks for listening," she said.

"Sure. But if you feel like that again, would you call me?"

"I don't know. I can't run to the phone every time I get a little melancholy."

"But when the melancholy seeps into despair, then you have to call, okay?"

"Okay."

"You're backing that promise with all the integrity of your soul, right?"

"Probably." Suzann wasn't meeting her eyes.

"I can't accept that."

"Okay. Okay. Three in the morning when I feel lonely I'll give you a call."

"What have I gotten myself into?"

Suzann had phoned Rose just once since then. Within twenty-five minutes, Rose was walking through the door with two pints of pralines 'n pecan ice cream. "Suzann," she was saying, "Now I'm not making this up because you need to hear something cheerful, but I overheard two girls talking about you the other day. Jill McMillan said, 'I was shocked to learn Suzann has a seven-year-old. She looks like she's just graduated from high school.'. . ."

Talking with Rose was like taking two aspirins when you had a fever. The virus still had to run its course, but you felt better. Then why shouldn't Suzann call Rose now? Because she had just left Rose thirty minutes ago. Besides, she was fine. Okay, so she'd thought about Peter for a few minutes; so she'd staged a memory that was still raw; so she'd remembered there was a pack of double-edged razor blades upstairs. She'd better call Rose.

"Rose? This is Suzann."

"Suzann. Did you forget something?"

"No. I want to forget something," answered Suzann. "Emotionally, I'm taking a nosedive."

"Oh, Suzann, I wish I could talk but I'm on my way to a meeting. Will you be okay? I'll save you a seat at church. And listen, if you promise not to think about Peter until then, I'll take you to a movie Tuesday night. I'll bring my neighbor to stay with your kids. She's great. She does dishes."

It was enough of a lift to jostle Suzann's mind into other directions. She hadn't seen a movie with an adult for a long time, and she looked forward to it like a young girl anticipating a slumber party.

Rose suggested a romantic thriller that Suzann had wanted to see.

"Can I go, too?" asked Trisha after Rose and her neighbor who did dishes had arrived. Suzann was stretching a plastic cover over a bowl of leftover potato-and-cheese soup.

"Not tonight."

"Oh, Mom." For a minute Trisha looked like she was going to kick the table leg.

Suzann stopped her with a glance. "This is just for grown-ups."

"That's me. Everyone always says, 'Man, how you've grown up!' "

"Yeah, but you still like to hear it," answered Suzann. "When someone claims you look older and you want to slap his face, that's when you'll be ready to go."

The show was a good choice. It had a strong plot and clever dialogue, and was laced with suspense. But it was not without flaws. Suzann pointed one out as they maneuvered through the parking lot.

"Did you notice that five minutes after Gloria had been fished out of the lake her hair looked like she'd just walked out of a beauty salon?"

Rose had noticed. "When they were giving her artificial respiration, they must have been near an electrical outlet so they could use a blow dryer and curling wand."

Suzann laughed. "Well, as long as she looked beautiful."

"Right. Sometimes you have to scrap other qualities for appearance." Rose paused, then added more quietly, "But maybe that's a trick they borrowed from real life."

19

"I'm not sure what you mean," said Suzann.

"Oh, something happened today and it's been on my mind." Rose was braking for a red light.

Suzann just watched her face. She wasn't going to prod unless it was necessary. It wasn't.

"It's a stupid thing. I was having lunch in the hospital cafeteria with a girl I've worked with. Natalie—you've seen her on the cover of *Vogue*. Not really *her*, but she's that striking. A doctor walked over to us, actually lifted Natalie's chin with his hand, and said, 'Weren't you working with me in the emergency room?' When Natalie just stared, he continued, 'Um, on the patient that caught his hand in the lawnmower.' Well, for the past two months Natalie has been in maternity. Do you know who works in emergency?"

"You."

"Me. And do you know who worked on the lawnmower victim with that doctor? Me. And do you know who was invisible at that table? Me."

Suzann didn't know what to say. Rose was the one who used words like a salve. And remembering the phrases Rose had rubbed into her own wounds, Suzann longed to reciprocate. But although she squeezed her mind for soothing words, nothing came out.

"I usually don't let things like this get to me," continued Rose. "I mean I grew up used to boys resisting being my partner. I know I'm not pretty. I could lose enough weight to make a twin sister. And my overbite—how many people's front teeth are the dominant feature in their profile?"

"Rose, they're not that bad."

"But usually I can counter my appearance by thinking about my strengths. I'm an excellent nurse. I do a good job as Relief Society president. I'm compassionate. I'm a terrific painter. I have a nice voice. A good sense of humor. I learn quickly . . ." Rose stopped and looked at Suzann. "I can have a list made up for you if you'd like—I didn't mean to brag. It's just that I've had a buoyant self-esteem, even though the outside of the ship is a little battered."

The car stopped in front of Suzann's home, but neither reached for a door handle. Rose went on. "Tonight I sat

20

leaning my elbows on the cold metal armrests, while Gloria up on the screen was nuzzled in Luke's warm embrace. And as he confessed all those things, like how beautiful she was and that he carried her image around in his mind and that he would love her for the rest of his life—it struck me. No one will ever talk to me that way. And those words—a handful of sentences—are what every girl in America grows up waiting to hear. She chooses her clothes and styles her hair and decorates her face and starves and sweats and does everything but carry a cue card to provoke those words. And if she's lucky enough to be reimbursed by the right man—if he declares her beauty and promises his love—those words become the crowning glory of her life. And even though they can't be kept in a treasure box, they are no less secure in the velvet casing of her memory, and can just as easily be taken out and cherished.

"But I've always told myself those words are just a media hype, capitalized on to sell shampoo and perfume and sometimes even window cleaner. And I told myself I didn't need them. That's what I thought . . . I thought I'd stopped jumping for the sour grapes."

Suzann wanted to embrace her, but she would have had to slide across the car seat. It would have been awkward. "Rose, you have qualities that transcend beauty. You influence people's lives. And looks—they change. When I look in the mirror, sometimes I'm pretty and sometimes I'm not. But even the most gorgeous women don't hold onto their beauty forever . . ." It didn't seem to be working. Suzann felt her words were as effective as a straw trying to mix cookie dough.

"It's okay. I know looks aren't everything. A person's value isn't measured just by a glass reflection. I've already worked through this stuff. My self-esteem will survive this jolt. Go on inside. See if your kids did okay. I'm fine."

Suzann hesitated a minute, but Rose was smiling her usual smile. She climbed out of the car. "You're better than fine, Rose. You're great. Really."

# 4

When Rose arrived home, she walked directly to the hall-light switch, fingering it gingerly before lifting up with a deliberateness more suited to launching a missile. The room exploded with light, as did the identical room in the mirror. Rose confronted her reflection. Her reflection. She had jousted with it all her life, and there it was again, trying to assume dominance, to usurp total definition of Rose Adams and poke the other invisible qualities into obscurity. No. She wouldn't let it. She slapped the switch back to darkness. By radar, Rose walked to the couch and fell into it. Still in her clothes, she stretched out and fused into the cushions. She was her own analyst.

Rose remembered a time when she would have bundled all her talents together and swapped them for beauty. She was in the eleventh grade, a junior in high school. . . .

Rose was a busy teenager, with friends and studies and projects and church activities. *But not with dates, thought* Rose. *Not with boys who wanted to show you off like an ornament on their arms or practice their kissing with you. Not with boys who kept boasting about how many tackles they made, or how many touchdown runs, or boys who could look into your eyes for fifty nights in a row and still not know who you were.* Rose left those boys to the other girls. And that was fine. There was only one man that really mattered, anyway.

"T. S." Simpson. Todd Salsbury. Alas, Mr. Simpson. He taught drama. No, he didn't teach it, he evoked it. He awakened his students' own natural delight in expression. He loosened one emotion and then another until what they could imagine, they could feel; and what they could feel, they could reflect. Like he himself did. When he stood in front of the class, they never knew if he was going to be Mr. Simpson the teacher or a hillbilly, a vengeful monarch, a domineering mother, or a used-car salesman. They never knew until he started to speak, with his lean body verifying the words in corresponding gestures.

But whatever his role, Rose could count on being spellbound by Mr. Simpson himself. His hair would be thick and dark with all the shadows of the night, and a little wild as though it couldn't be completely subdued by a comb. And after he laughed, a loud laugh that echoed off the walls, he would softly bite his lower lip for maybe three seconds before assuming his next expression. And she knew that she would be watching his blue eyes, so undiluted that all the other colors in the room seemed to fade. She'd be watching those eyes and waiting for a chance to intercept the electric current of his gaze. And so would most of the other girls.

It was obvious he had a following of female students. After teaching only eight weeks, he had to switch his phone number to "unlisted" because he was getting hundreds of calls and only a few hello's. Before his classes, bathroom mirrors were invaded by girls with brushes and mascara wands and tiny jars of lip gloss. After his classes, Mr. Simpson was invaded with questions. "What are some good plays to read?" asked Susie Martin, who wasn't keeping up with their current reading assignments. "If you were really serious about acting, which university would be best?" Bernice Evans wanted to know, even though she would be lucky if her parents could afford the local junior college.

If some of the girls were obvious, no one was blatant enough to confess, "I love Mr. Simpson." No, when they talked about him they used sentences like, "I wonder if he dates," and "What kind of person do you think he would marry?" And some girls adored him without ever mentioning his name. But it was obvious which ones he affected. When he recited a passage even vaguely romantic, they came out of class in a trance.

Not just a few of them, either; and some were very pretty. And that's why and when Rose needed to be beautiful.

See, maybe if she were exquisite enough, he would be drawn to her. He would try to find a reason to keep her after school. Maybe he would ask her to read a script with him—to see if it was something he'd want to put on, he'd explain. And at just past three, she'd enter the drama room, a perfect stage now that all the subordinate characters had been dismissed. They'd sit down in chairs that almost touched and read lines from the same page. But suddenly she'd look up and those blue eyes would be fastened on her face and he would ignore his cue for a minute, then apologize and go on, but before long she would catch him studying her again. She would feel self-conscious and blush a soft pink shade over her high, sculptured cheekbones, and he would say, "I'm sorry; I can't concentrate. I shouldn't have asked you to come." And she would just look at him, through eyes resting under shades of thick, curling lashes, not muddy like her real eyes, but as green as summer grass. And he would tell her it was so hard for him to pretend that she was just like one of the other students, when her very presence tempted him to take her in his arms . . . and then he would. And he'd kiss her. Forever. Maybe that's what would happen, if she were beautiful enough.

So for the first time in her life, Rose turned down desserts. She chose clothes in shades that were supposed to enhance her coloring and she bought makeup from under the counter, demonstrated by saleswomen, instead of the kind encased in plastic on a display rack. But the real transformation would come when she had her prominent front teeth pulled back into line. Her parents regretted not having had the overbite taken care of three years before, when metal smiles were familiar in Rose's group, but they couldn't afford it then, just as they couldn't afford it now. Yet when Rose told them she was saving the money herself, they said they would match her half with their own. Maybe by summer vacation she would have her braces earned.

An attractive Rose was imminent, but it didn't take the total metamorphosis to attract Mr. Simpson's attention. He frequently called on her to recite a section from a play, urging the class to watch her expression and listen to the inflections of her voice. He even suggested she audition for a part in his first-semester production of *Our Town* as one of the mothers; she did, and was chosen. Rose slid into her character deftly, and after her performances, Mr. Simpson smiled as he told her she had done well.

That's why she intended to try out for the next play, *Cinderella*. Rose didn't for a minute think of herself in the starring role. Okay, she imagined being Cinderella once or twice, but she knew it was a fantasy and there was no magic wand to make it come true. But it wouldn't take supernatural powers to land the role of fairy godmother. It wasn't going to fall in her lap, but if she could resurrect from her childhood memories that magic grandmother with the stardust dress and eyes that twinkled out solutions, maybe Rose could bring her to life and win the part.

But she never got the chance to prove herself fairy godmother material. Rose lost her wisdom teeth and the opportunity to audition in the same week. And as she lay in bed with a chipmunk mouth, she wondered if there wasn't something she could still do to be involved with the play . . . with Mr. Simpson. She would offer to work on scenery.

"Mr. Simpson?" Rose went into drama early the day she returned to school.

"Rose." Mr. Simpson was looking through some papers. "I thought you would be trying out for the play."

"I was sick. I had my wisdom teeth pulled."

"That's right. You weren't in class, either."

"But I'd still like to be involved with the play—with *Cinderella*. I'd like to help with the scenery."

"No, Rose. I'd rather you didn't work on the scenery."

Had he slapped her face? Or could the words really startle her that much? "I'm not a bad painter."

"I'd like you to be in the play."

"But it's already been cast."

Mr. Simpson put aside his papers and blinded her with the blue of his eyes. "I've saved you a part."

If his earlier words had surprised her, these were like bubbles coming out of his mouth.

He continued. "I'd like you to play Drizella."

"The ugly stepsister?"

"Yes. One of the stepsisters."

"You had me picked out for the ugly stepsister?"

"It should be a fun role. You'll enjoy it."

Had it been any other part, or offered by any other drama teacher, she would have danced all the way home instead of crying. She should have been flattered. By holding open the stepsister role, Mr. Simpson was making a bold affirmation of her acting abilities. But just as loudly, he was declaring she was ugly.

Rose's mother noticed the tears and sat with her daughter on the couch.

"What is it, honey?"

"I'm ugly, Mom."

"You're not. You've been such a sweet daughter."

"Mom, I could be a saint, but it doesn't show up in the mirror."

"You're not ugly. You've lost over ten pounds; you're looking so much better." Her mother reached for her face. "It's your teeth, isn't it? We should have had those fixed. We'll get them fixed. We'll make an appointment. I'll take money out of the new car fund. This is more important."

"No."

"Yes, Rose. We should have done this a long time ago."

"No!" She looked at her mother. The tears were solidifying into resolve. "I don't want braces any more. Maybe I'm not pretty, but that's not all there is. I'll show him. I mean, you'll see."

Rose had never been as nervous as when the curtain started limping up on act one. There were a trillion dancing molecules agitating inside her body, and she could feel them all. It was their first performance, almost like another dress rehearsal, put on for the student body during the last hours of school. Rose wanted to run offstage, run home, run back to when she was a little girl and there was no anxiety too large to be swallowed in her mother's lap. She couldn't go through with it. But she'd have to; she'd already committed herself. Each line was implanted in her mind. The old lines, which she had practiced over and over with the cast, and also the new lines that she had practiced over and over in the mirror. The lines that no one would expect.

Drizella, her sister Anastasia, and their mother were traipsing across the mansion floor, which Cinderella was still scrubbing. They stopped before the maiden in rags. The mother sneered, "This will have to be redone."

Cinderella looked up beseechingly, but her guardian had already turned away. Drizella was suppose to say, "And when you're finished here, I have some mending I want done." Instead, Rose replied, "It could be worse, Cinderella. You could be scrubbing on a dirt floor."

Cinderella gave Rose a startled look and the audience laughed.

In Drizella's next scene, she was sitting at a wooden table with her sister and mother while Cinderella served them porridge for lunch.

"It tastes like you cooked this too long," snarled the mother. "What do you think, girls?"

"It's awful," answered Anastasia, between big, slurping gulps.

Drizella was only expected to echo Anastasia's distaste. Instead, she answered, "Let's toss it and send out for a pizza."

Rose got more laughs. From the audience, not the cast.

There was a knock on the door.

"What are you waiting for, Cinderella?" barked her stepmother. "Answer it!"

In a velvet coat and coiffured wig stood the royal messenger.

"You wouldn't happen to have a pizza?" asked Drizella.

He scowled at her and started to unfurl his scroll. "I have a message. Tomorrow night, the king is holding a ball to find a wife for the prince. He requests the presence of every maiden in the village."

The mother's eyes blazed. "We shall surely be there— right, girls?"

Drizella was only supposed to nod eagerly, but Rose turned to the messenger and replied, "Before I commit myself, can you give me an idea of what the refreshments will be like?"

The other actors gave Rose a "what's-going-on?" stare. The messenger paused and walked away without responding.

The mother volleyed her gaze from Drizella to Anastasia. "I wonder which of you the prince will choose."

"He will choose me," burst Anastasia.

Drizella was suppose to argue, "No, me!" Instead she said, "Let's offer him both of us. We could be a package deal, but he'd have to decide within the fortnight or the special would be off."

The mother shook her head, but was ready with her next line. "Cinderella will have to get busy on the dresses."

Again, Drizella deviated from the script. "Go ahead and make me a size seven, Cinderella. I'm going on a crash diet. I think I can lose 35 pounds by tomorrow night."

After her exit, Rose grabbed the ball dress she would be wearing in her next scene and hid inside folds of the curtain. Here she slipped the gown over her clothes and pinned up her hair, attaching the hideous ribbon that was part of her costume.

At the ball, the prince was being introduced to the sisters.

"How do you do, sire?" smiled Anastasia, with eyelashes flapping as though they were about to fly away.

Drizella should have added, "I'm most delighted to meet you." But that's not what Rose had in mind.

"Haven't I seen you somewhere before?" Drizella was studying the prince. She snapped her fingers. "We were dating in the pre-existence."

The audience, like many Mesa audiences, was filled with Mormons. The line got a laugh.

Again, Rose sneaked from the stage to her hiding place to change for her final scene. The play seemed to be going in fast forward. On again.

At their door was the duke, making the rounds with a glass slipper. He tried Anastasia, but no amount of prying could ease the foot inside. Then he turned to Drizella.

"Look," she said. "I can't try that shoe on if you don't have one of those little nylon socks. Frankly, it isn't sanitary. But trust me. I'm the one the prince has been looking for."

The cast was getting used to Rose's deviations, and the audience loved them. A practically unfazed Cinderella walked in and claimed the shoe, reinforcing her words with a perfect fit. Now she and the prince could live happily ever after. But what about Rose?

No more hiding. She stood backstage with the rest of the cast. They made a circle around her and started to ask questions, but were interrupted by Mr. Simpson's slicing command. "Rose. Come with me."

"Let her do it like that tonight," someone called, but he was already making quick strides to the drama room. Rose had to jog to keep up. Inside, the door barely cleared her when he jerked it shut.

He spun to face her. His hair was a little more wild than usual, his eyes more intense. They were alone—but this was not the fantasy.

"What did you think you were doing? What gave you the right to change a play we've been working on for over a month? I was ready to walk out there and yank you off the stage. Where did you hide between acts?"

Rose could feel the tears, smell the tears, taste the tears, and when she spoke she could hear the tears. "I'm sorry, I won't mess it up tonight."

Her conciliatory anguish took the edge off his rage. "What made you do it, Rose? What made you do it?"

"After I thought about it, I wanted to show that even though Drizella wasn't pretty, she was lovable," Rose replied. "But at first I wanted to hurt you."

He stretched closer, as though the answer were in fine print to be read on her face. "Why would you want to hurt me?" His words were soft now.

"Because you hurt me."

"I've never done anything to hurt you, Rose."

"You mean more to me than anyone in the world," she explained, "and to you, I am ugly."

"You're not ugly. I never said you were ugly . . . because of the part? The stepsister part?" He dropped his head back and moaned. "How many female parts were there? Next to Cinderella, you had as many lines as anyone, except maybe the stepmother. I put you in that play because you're special. I see qualities in you that are usually missing in beautiful girls. You're sensitive and responsive, and when you play a part, you *are* that part. Rose, don't handicap yourself by believing that appearance is the thing that matters. It's not. It's really not."

He clasped his hand above her wrist, as though it weren't enough for her to hear the words; they had to diffuse from his skin into hers.

For the first time, Rose lifted her head. His eyes were so close. She was being sucked up into them. But no, she had to concentrate. She must record everything about this moment because she would be playing it over and over again.

Mr. Simpson continued, "You're clever and imaginative and have a heck of a lot of nerve. But if you *ever* change your lines like that again, you won't walk off that stage alive."

Rose would give the right lines, but his threat didn't worry her. Even if she died this minute, it wouldn't matter. He had said she was special. He had said she had things most beautiful girls didn't. And he had touched her arm. Touched her arm and touched her mind with the determination that looks weren't going to be important.

# 5

Unlike Rose, Carolyn had never faced a showdown with the girl in the mirror. As she was growing up, her greatest physical obstacle had been deciding whether or not to have her hair cut. There were advantages to being attractive. People remembered your name and were eager to be your friend. Carolyn appreciated the edge that it often provided. But pretty wasn't getting her anywhere now with her nephew Tyler. He was too young and too related.

Carolyn was kneeling by the bathtub with a bottle of baby shampoo. She could feel water soaking into the knees of her jeans. "Tyler, Grandma said I had to wash your hair. You've been here almost a week and we haven't washed it once."

"But I've been swimming; that's the same thing."

"Unless you were swimming in shampoo, it's not the same thing. Lie back and get your hair wet."

"No. At home my mom washes my hair in the sink. She has a sprayer that comes out so I don't get water in my eyes."

"I remember. You've told me three times about the sprayer. But we don't have one. If I were a plumber I'd be installing one right now, but I'm not. You're stuck with the bathtub faucet."

"I won't lie down."

"Tyler, I'm going to wash your hair. If you want to sit up while I pour a pitcher of water over your head, that's fine."

"I'm not lying down."

"Okay." Carolyn dashed to the kitchen. The messy kitchen. Her parents had left early for a dinner party, and she had been the cook. She had made spaghetti. While Josh, the youngest, played in the cupboards, Tyler and Janice had helped, measuring ingredients, stirring the sauce, and dropping the noodles—carefully—into boiling water. Not until Carolyn had set their bowls before them did they insist they didn't like spaghetti. Tyler wanted chicken noodle soup. Carolyn heated it. Janice didn't like soup. Carolyn made her a peanut butter and jelly sandwich. Josh wanted some of everything. In less than ninety minutes the kitchen had gone from clean to chaotic. Carolyn hadn't had the chance to clean it yet. She still didn't. She grabbed the pitcher and sprinted down the hall.

One step inside the bathroom and her heel caught the edge of a puddle. Before she could grab the counter, she was down. From the floor it looked as though either Tyler had drowned or the bathtub was empty. She suspected the later, which was verified as she climbed to her feet. Following a trail of soaked carpet, Carolyn stalked Tyler to the linen closet, where he was sandwiched on a shelf of clean sheets.

"Come out of there!" she barked.

"Please don't wash my hair. I can't stand it when water gets in my eyes."

"Obviously it doesn't bother you when water gets all over the house. And on the sheets . . . those will have to be stuck in the dryer." Carolyn sighed. Of course, this *would* happen tonight when she had so much to do. "Go put your pajamas on. Then you're helping me in the bathroom until we have dry land in there again."

Tyler, who just the night before had spent thirty-five minutes getting ready for bed, was instantly in his pajamas and next to Carolyn, sponging water with a towel.

"Janice and Josh have been asleep for an hour," Carolyn said. "When we're finished, I think it will be time for you to go to bed, too."

"But they're just kids. That's why they went to bed early."

"Once you get past three-and-a-half feet I guess you're not a kid anymore. Well, even grown-ups like you and me need sleep."

"Would you read me a story on the couch first?" asked Tyler.

"I have to read a chapter in the history of Western civilization for class tomorrow; will that do?"

"What's it about?"

"Never mind. There aren't a lot of pictures." Carolyn wrung her sopping towel into the tub. "You want one story? You promise just one? You tricked me last night. If you ask for two, can I have your hot wheels racer?"

"Girls don't play with cars."

"Why not? When they're sixteen they get to drive, too. Haven't you heard about the women's liberation movement? In the 1980s girls play with cars. When they grow up they work construction, go to law school, sit on boards of directors, and become journalists."

"My mom doesn't do all those things." Tyler wrung his towel into the tub as he had seen Carolyn do.

"I know. She changes diapers and cooks and cleans and washes and, if she has some spare time, cans fruit."

"Yeah. And she reads stories."

Carolyn smiled at Tyler—the first real smile since he had fled from his bath. "Some liberated women read stories, too. Go get me one. After I change I'll meet you on the couch."

Tyler popped up and started to run away.

"Not a library," Carolyn called after him. "One."

When Carolyn opened "Three Billy Goats Gruff" into both of their laps and started to read, she was thinking about a game adapted from that story which she had played as a little girl. Her father would be the troll, lying on the living-room floor, and as goats, she and her sisters would try to run by him without being caught. But he could snatch so quickly, even when he didn't seem to be watching. Before Carolyn could detect the shift of a muscle she would be in his grasp, and he would tuck her securely under an arm or leg while he baited another goat. Sometimes he had all three of his daughters. The only way they could get loose was by touching his nose, immediately putting the troll into a deep sleep. Or by saying they had to go to the bathroom.

"No!" said Tyler.

"What's the matter?"

"You're not reading it right."

"Oh? Am I reading it backwards? Upside down?"

"No. When the little goat talks you're supposed to talk"—Tyler's voice raised an octave—"real high. Make the goats sound like they really would."

"Like they really would? Okay. Then the little goat said, 'Naaa naaa.' "

Tyler gave her a bewildered look.

"That's what a goat would really sound like," Carolyn explained. "Wait! I've got it. When I come to the goats' and troll's parts, you can talk for them. You can make their voices just how you want. Won't that be fun?"

"No. I don't remember what they say."

"You must have read this story a hundred times. If you can remember building a sandcastle on the beach with your mom over two years ago, surely you can remember what the goats say."

"I miss my mom."

"You'll see her on Saturday. That's not tomorrow, but the next day," answered Carolyn. "Look, if you really don't want to be the goats, I'll make their voices how you want them."

"No. I just want my mom." He started to cry.

"Tyler, don't cry. I'll sing the voices. I'll get down on my hands and knees and act out the story for you."

"No. Go away."

"Go away? Here I am straining my creativity to please you, and you tell me to go away? If somebody goes it will be you—to your bed."

Tyler started to wail.

"Tyler, you're going to wake up Janice and Josh. If you wake them up, I'll kill you."

Tyler howled louder. So loudly they could barely hear the doorbell ring.

Carolyn opened the door to Jesse, leaning on one arm against the wall. Instantly she regretted the fact that this was the night she'd have to let the air out of their relationship. He could look more sauve in jeans and a polo shirt than most guys looked in a three-piece suit.

She didn't have to ask him in; they had been seeing each other too much for the opened door not to be invitation enough. And she didn't have to tell him her evening was running amuck. Her smile said it. Instead of her usual grin—a jaunty mixture of delight and amusement—she merely lifted the corners of her mouth. And then there were the sobs coming from the background.

"Am I interrupting the party?" he asked gently.

"Yes. It's a lynching party. Only Tyler and I can't decide who gets to lynch first," replied Carolyn. "Tyler refused to let me wash his hair, then he bolted from the tub and hid in the linen closet, getting water all over everything. He wouldn't go to bed without a story, which I couldn't read right, and now he's crying for his mom. And all evening long I've been haunted by a messy kitchen and a history reading assignment."

Jesse burst into Mighty Mouse's theme song: "Here I come to save the day . . ."

He put his hands on Carolyn's shoulders and turned her in the direction of her room. "Go read your history. I'll take care of Tyler."

"No." She resisted his manipulation. "He's probably tired. Maybe he'd let me rock him to sleep."

"Carolyn, go read." Jesse nudged her towards her room and went to Tyler, still whimpering on the couch.

Jesse patted his leg. "Tyler, you need a story."

"I don't want a story. I want my mom."

"Okay, but this is a special story."

"What's special about it?"

"Come with me and I'll show you." Jesse led Tyler into the living room and shut the sliding doors behind them. They sat together on the piano bench.

"I don't want to read a piano book." Tyler was wrinkling his nose.

"We're not using a book. You know what dwarfs are, don't you? Like in *Snow White*?"

"Yeah. They're kids with grown-up faces."

Jesse laughed. "That sounds like a pretty good description. I'm going to play a story about dwarfs on the piano. You'll be able to hear them as they hike through the forest. Sometimes it will almost sound like they're running as they go up and down the hills—like this . . ."

Jesse made short runs up and down the scale.

"There will be other places that are so steep the dwarfs will have to slide down. Then it will sound like this . . ." Jesse's fingers skipped down the keyboard. "I want you to listen for that." Jesse played it again.

"After they travel for a while," Jesse continued, "the music will get heavier. They'll be pushing through some thick growth—trees and shrubs. See if you can tell when they're doing that. Then they'll scurry over more hills and do some more sliding until it sounds deep again. That's because they'll be in the thickest part of the forest. And after they go just a little ways, they'll peer through the branches into a clearing, an open place with grass, and there . . . they'll see something magical."

"What is it?"

"You'll have to wait and find out."

Jesse started the dwarfs on their march. His left hand kept a steady rhythm while his right hand traipsed up and down the keys.

"Can you see them?" Jesse asked. "The path is narrow. Only bits of blue sky filter through the leaves; everything else is green. Not green like an idle TV screen or a dollar bill, but green like a bright frozen pea."

"Are the tree trunks green?"

"The only defect in the story and you pick up on it. Okay, the trunks are brown, but they're almost hidden by the leaves."

"Do the dwarfs have on long caps that hang to their shoulders?"

"You can see them, too, huh?" confirmed Jesse. "Listen. Can you tell when they start to slide?"

"Now?"

"Not yet."

"Now?"

"Yep. That was one. Here come the others."

Tyler, imagining the dwarfs sliding, almost wiggled off the piano bench. "It sounds deeper," he said. "Are they almost to the open place?"

36

"The trees are getting thicker. They have to use their hands to spread a path through the branches. But they have some more hills and sliding to do before they get to the clearing."

Tyler caught the music scaling down. "They're sliding again. They're stirring up so much dust and leaves I can hardly breathe."

Jesse laughed. "Now listen. It's going to get deeper."

"Are they at the clearing?"

Jesse changed from the marching rhythm to a light, ethereal melody. It reminded Tyler of the sounds he heard when he opened his mother's music box.

"What's in the clearing? What do they see?"

"Fairies," answered Jesse. "The girls' dresses are made out of rose petals and the boys are dressed in green like leprechauns. Can you see them dancing? Some aren't even touching the ground."

"Do they have wings, then?"

"Of course. The wings are transparent, like thin glass, and when they catch the sunlight they glitter in a rainbow of colors."

"Oh, I wish I could hold one," said Tyler.

"Uh-oh."

"What's happening?"

"They're scampering away." Jesse's fingers were skipping up the keyboard.

"Why?" asked Tyler. "Didn't they want the dwarfs to watch them?"

"No. Fairies are very shy."

"I don't want them to go."

"Two will come back. The fairy prince and the fairy princess."

Tyler recognized the music box again. "There they are. The princess is the most beautifullest, huh? And the prince is the strongest."

"You could be right."

"They must not be afraid of the dwarfs."

"They're bolder, but they'll be going away, too."

"There they go," said Tyler, when Jesse started playing up the scale.

"There they go," echoed Jesse. "Now the dwarfs are going to march back."

"It sounds like the beginning."

"You're right. You have a good ear."

"I don't have two good ears?"

"That's just an expression they use when you have a feel for music."

"Oh. What are the dwarfs doing now?"

"You tell me," said Jesse.

"They're going up and down the hills."

"That's right."

"Make them go back and watch the fairies."

"They can't."

"Why not?"

"They have to go back to their cottage and do their work," explained Jesse.

"What work?"

"Well, they got up this morning and had a huge breakfast —toast and eggs and ham and muffins and hashbrown potatoes and bacon and oatmeal. And then they left without cleaning up the kitchen. It's a disaster."

"Oh."

"Now listen; they're coming inside. They're going to shut the door." Two final chords. "Boom, boom."

"It would be fun to be a dwarf and live in the forest with the fairies," said Tyler.

"Why don't we pretend that we're dwarfs? We can march into the kitchen and straighten it up."

"Okay."

"Remember to lift your legs up high. And keep your eyes open for mushrooms."

Jesse and Tyler stomped into the kitchen.

"I'll put things away," said Jesse. "Can you stack the dishes in the sink and rinse them? I'll get you the stool from the pantry. A real dwarf would have to stand on a stool, too."

Carolyn had heard the music from her room. Why would Jesse play the piano? She couldn't believe Tyler would be interested in that. Four-year-olds just don't lose themselves in classical music. But the piece was compelling and Carolyn interrupted her reading to listen.

She imagined Jesse's fingers stroking the keys. Fingers that were used to playing a computer keyboard found a piano keyboard also accommodating. She'd watched those fingers balance a spinning softball, cut up a green salad, hold a fuzzy caterpillar, and flick water at her from a fountain. She'd seen them black after digging into the guts of her car. She'd felt his fingers twist her hair, ski down her cheek, outline her lips. And she'd felt their warmth when they reached for her hand.

Why did she have to tell those fingers to loosen their grip? Because if she didn't, they'd pull her into a world where the smell of a dirty diaper penetrated the air more often than the sound of the number-one hit record, where washing hair was as easy as talking a bird down from a tree, and where clothes hampers generated dirty laundry like the storybook pot which wouldn't stop making porridge. Jesse's fingers would pull her away from her dreams—dreams she'd lived with much longer than she'd lived with thoughts of Jesse. She owed allegiance to them. Which meant she should be studying. Carolyn returned to Joan of Arc, a woman with conviction.

It was nice that the drama of the Western world could be tucked into neat little chapters. And it was nice to finish reading an assignment, close the book, and put the chapters away. Carolyn stood up and started to stretch.

"Carolyn!" Tyler was approaching her door. When she opened it and started out, he ran into her.

"Carolyn! Come with me. I want to show you something."

She followed him through the family room, where Jesse was reading the paper, and into the kitchen. It was clean. Almost as clean as if she'd tackled it herself.

"Did you guys do this?" She gave Tyler a hug. "You're wonderful!"

Tyler's smile was almost too big for his face.

"If we had known you were so good with dishes, we would have put you on the clean-up crew earlier," Carolyn said. "Anyone who works so hard earns a piece of chocolate cake."

"Don't get any crumbs on the counter," Tyler warned, as he started to climb up a stool.

After she had set Tyler's cake in front of him, Carolyn took a piece in to Jesse.

"Thanks," she told him. "You certainly know how to rescue a maiden in distress. Do I have to give you my firstborn child, or would you settle for a piece of cake?"

"I'll take the cake tonight. After I slay the dragon, I'll ask for your child."

"Carolyn!" Tyler was calling her from the kitchen. "Can I finish the rest of my cake for breakfast? I'm ready to go to bed."

"I'll save your cake for you, but you'll have to take it up with Grandma whether it can be breakfast or not."

Tyler climbed down from his stool and shuffled over to them. "Could I have Jesse tuck me in?"

Jesse set his unfinished cake on the end table and turned to Carolyn. "If you touch my cake while I'm gone, you'll be in big trouble."

Carolyn traced the diamond designs in the couch with her finger while she waited for Jesse to return. *How will I bring it up?* she wondered anxiously. She tried out some leads: "Jesse, remember when I told you I wasn't ready to get married . . . I'm getting too serious . . . Would you mind if we picked things up in about four years?"

Jesse was back, finishing his cake. She couldn't spring it on him while he was eating. She'd wait awhile.

"I liked your song on the piano," she told him, after he had turned down an offer for more cake. "But how did you get Tyler to listen?"

"That was the 'March of the Dwarfs' by Edvard Grieg. When I was learning it in grade school, I made up a story to go with the music. That's what I told Tyler."

"Will you tell me the story?"

"I have to tell it to you on the piano."

They migrated to the living room.

Jesse explained about the dwarfs and the fairies as he matched their actions to music.

Carolyn was fascinated. "No wonder Tyler listened," she said. "You make me wish I hadn't quit taking piano lessons. Will you play another song?"

40

"Okay." Jesse studied the lattice pattern on the empty music stand for a moment before putting pressure to the keys. Then his nimble fingers danced over them, drawing forth a sweet, poignant melody.

The music played like a love sonnet. It mingled with Carolyn's blood and swept through her veins until she could feel it in every part of her body. It was a drug that made her feel lightheaded and buoyant. It stimulated pleasant visions of lakes in the park and candy-colored clouds and women with flowing sunshine hair and lacy dresses dancing with tall, handsome men . . . who looked like Jesse. When the music ended, Carolyn felt as though an exhilarating speedboat ride had jerked to a stop.

"That was beautiful," she said. "What's it called? Did you think of a story to go with it?"

"It's called 'Liebestraum'—'A Dream of Love.' I memorized it in the ninth grade. When I was learning it, I didn't think of a story. I was imagining you."

Carolyn wasn't sure the effects of the song had worn off yet. Why would that confession make her want to cry? Oh, yes. Because she was going to shift their relationship into low gear tonight. Maybe she would save that for next time.

# 6

While Carolyn was struggling with her commitment to put the brakes on a relationship, Suzann was contemplating how to recharge one that had stalled.

Casual. Being casual is the key, Suzann told herself as she joined the stream of rush-hour traffic. *Pouncing on Peter won't work; he mustn't think that I'm waiting here with a big steel trap to snare him. Nor is he to suspect that I've been keeping my heart on "hold" until he's ready to join me. The projected image must be Suzann White sitting down to a feast of life, heaping my plate with adventure, romance, and fulfillment. I'm planning my trip to the Orient. Gorgeous, wealthy men are continually sending me roses, offering me jewelry, and inviting me for rides in their private planes. My best-selling novel is under final negotiations with a major publishing company. Maybe the details aren't exact, but that's the image. Peter needs to get the idea I could take him or leave him. No. He has to know that I would take him, but I don't need him. I have to show him in some subtle way that the door he's shut isn't locked.*

Timing. *Timing is crucial,* Suzann decided. She was looking at the clouds instead of the left-turn arrow as it flashed green; the car behind her honked. It wasn't a "Hey-you-idiot-some-of-us-don't-want-to-sit-here-all-day" honk; it was more like, "Excuse me, but the arrow." *On Friday afternoons, drivers start unwinding for the weekend. They tend to be more indulgent. If you're going to miss a green arrow, do it on a Friday afternoon. If you're going to crack open the door for Peter, when do you do it? When he's becoming disenchanted with Marta: after he discovers she doesn't know how to make tender pie crust, or that she's been stealing his sales ideas and presenting them as her own, or that she's murdered someone. That's the time to put the welcome mat out.*

But how could Suzann know when Marta's flaws were emerging like mold on a piece of old bread? It wasn't as if she received progress reports on their relationship. And she couldn't exactly decode Peter's love life from his honk when he arrived for the children. How would she know when the time was right?

Suzann pulled into the drive of the house that sheltered her children on weekdays. Trisha and Kevin were already bolting from the front door to greet her.

"Do you have everything? Kevin, go get your shoes," called Suzann.

"And my picture, too," Kevin yelled back on his way into the house.

Trisha climbed into the car. "Hi, Mom. The hamster got out of its cage today and the cat caught him and ate him."

"That's a good lesson. Sometimes things that seem to confine us are for our own protection."

"What?"

"Open the door for Kevin."

"Hi, Mom."

"Hi, Kevin. How was your day?" Suzann was backing into the street.

"Okay," Kevin answered. "The hamster got loose and the cat ate him."

"I know. Trisha told me. Did anything else happen worth mentioning?"

"I made you a picture." Kevin held it in front of Suzann's face.

"Move it! I can't see the road!" When her visibility was restored, Suzann took a deep breath. "Just tell me about it now, Kevin. I'll look at it when we get home."

"It's pictures of me helping you. Here I'm opening a jar of

pickles. We were gonna have to go out to eat if I didn't open it. But I did. And there I'm carrying in the groceries. See that sack?"

Suzann glanced over quickly and then returned her eyes to the traffic. "The one with the teeth on the top?"

"Not teeth, ridges, like real sacks have. Well, in there is a big bag of Reese's Pieces."

"Reese's Pieces? And you guys didn't rip them open on the way home and spill them all over the back seat?"

"Mom, they were in the trunk. And here in the corner I'm pouring some medicine down the sink because it's clogged up. See, I'm doing all the things a daddy does. I'll be the daddy. You don't need to worry about anything."

"You're a little boy, Kevin," argued Trisha. "You can't be the daddy."

"Uh-huh! I'm gonna take care of Mom. I'm gonna be the daddy."

"Little boys can't be daddies."

"Okay, okay," Suzann interrupted. "Kevin, I'm glad you want to help. That makes me happy. Trisha, what did you talk about in school today?"

"Nothing. Oh, yeah. Families. We even talked about families like ours."

"Like ours?"

"Yeah. Families where the kids lived with just a mom or a dad."

"Oh. Broken families."

"No. Not broken families. That wasn't the name. It was singing parent families."

"Singing parent families?" Suzann chuckled. "Do you mean single-parent families?"

"Yeah."

"Did you remember your dad is picking you up tonight? He should be here about six, within an hour, so the first thing I want you both to do when we get home is pack, okay? Pajamas, toothbrushes, clean clothes. Are you supposed to bring anything special?"

"Maybe we should bring our church clothes. I think daddy's going to start coming to church."

44

Suzann risked taking her eyes off the road for several seconds as she studied Trisha's face. "What makes you say that?"

"Because the last time we stayed with Dad, we went to the mall and he tried on church clothes."

Suzann pulled into the parking space marked with the signature of her Chevette—several puddles of oil.

"We'll wait until Dad asks for the church clothes," she said as they walked into their home. "But he'll probably want your swimsuits."

Suzann relaxed on the couch with the newspaper while Trisha and Kevin gathered their things. Trisha came down first. "I wish you didn't have to stay alone."

Suzann dropped the paper and pulled Trisha next to her on the couch. "Thanks, Trisha, but I'll be okay."

"What are you going to do for dinner?"

"I don't know. The ward is having a progressive dinner."

"I've never eaten progressives."

Suzann laughed. "A progressive dinner is when you eat an appetizer at one place, a salad at another, the main course at the next place, and the dessert somewhere else."

"That sounds like fun."

"It might be fun, but I'm tired tonight. I'll probably just fix something here."

"You know what kind of dinner sounds the funnest to me?"

"Most fun. What?"

"A dinner with me and Kevin and you and dad. All of us again."

Suzann smiled, but it was a consolation-prize smile. She straightened the clips in Trisha's hair.

"It seems funny when you're not there," continued Trisha. "Dad cuts everything in pieces for us. Even bananas and pizza. About the only thing he doesn't cut up is soup. And he asks so many questions about school. I thought he asked because he'd never been but then he told me he had and I said it must have been a long time ago for him to forget so much and he said it was . . . And I'd just like another girl at the table."

"Doesn't Marta eat with you?"

"She used to. But I haven't seen her for a long time. Not last time or even the time before. Maybe Dad has stopped liking her. He used to ask if we would mind having Marta for another mom, but he doesn't anymore."

*Timing is crucial,* thought Suzann. *Is it D-day? Has the mold surfaced? Is Peter waiting for a welcome mat?*

"I think a dinner with you and me and Kevin and Dad might be the best kind of dinner, too," said Suzann. "Should I see if Dad wants to bring you back early Sunday and we can all eat together?"

"Yes! Yes, ask him!"

The doorbell rang.

"That's him!" cried Trisha, jumping for the door.

"Dad!" yelled Kevin, as he skipped down the stairs with his duffel bag. Kevin must have been getting over his obsession to answer the door, because when Trisha pulled it open he didn't howl.

"Oh, Mark," said Trisha. "We thought you were our dad."

"I just got a new bike!" exclaimed a little boy with as much pride as any man who had just purchased a sports car. "Can you come and see it?"

"Well, we're waiting for our dad, but he's not here yet." Trisha turned back to the couch. "Can we go, Mom, if we hurry?"

"If you hurry."

A silence that foreshadowed the quiet of the weekend to come was trapped inside with the slamming of the front door. Suzann couldn't remember which story she had been reading in the paper. Was it the one about the skyrocketing hospital costs, or the one about plummeting education funds? It didn't matter. There was a new focal point and it was out the front window and it was candy apple red and it was a Mazda. Peter was here. Peter was not only here; he was getting out of his car. So this was going to be another exception to the rule. In the two years of every-other-weekend custody, only rarely did Peter opt for the doorbell when he could summon his wards with a honk.

Suzann walked to the front door and waited for it to ring. And when it did, she waited longer so it wouldn't seem as though she was standing behind it.

46

"The kids are down a few doors looking at a new bike," Suzann explained, after she and Peter had exchanged flickering smiles. "Would you like to come in and wait?"

"Sure. I wanted to see you, anyway."

They stood several feet apart, studying each other as if they were creatures who spoke with their thoughts and listened with their eyes. Time didn't freeze. It reached backwards, pulling forth crisp images of younger Peters, younger Suzanns. Images surprisingly ordinary—Peter leaving for work, waving with his eyebrows so Kevin wouldn't hear his good-bye and cling like an appendage to his leg; Suzann dancing to the radio as she picked up blocks and socks, straightened cushions, and tossed trinkets into the toy basket.

"Sometimes," said Peter, "It seems like I'm on vacation and this is still home."

"Does it? Maybe you should be sending some postcards."

Peter smiled. "Are you doing as wonderful as you look?"

Being casual is the key. "I don't know. Let me go check the mirror."

"I say you look great. Any mirror that says something different is a liar."

"Thanks. How are you?"

"Good. I'm doing real good."

"Work?"

"It's good, too. How about your work?"

"We've ordered a word processing computer," answered Suzann. "Do you know what that means? Mistakes and revisions can be altered on the screen before printing. No more liquid paper. Only I think I'll keep some of the correction fluid around in case dull white fingernail polish ever becomes the rage."

"On top of technology, on top of fashion."

"Not on top. Just caught up in the stream." Suzann realized they were still standing. "Would you like to sit down? I don't know what's keeping Trisha and Kevin. Maybe Mark's family is having something delicious for supper and they decided to stay."

Peter laughed, and they both took a seat on the couch.

"I can't think of anything more delicious than your barbecued ribs," he said.

"Those always were your favorite. I was going to fix them Sunday night. Why don't you bring the kids back early and we can have dinner together?"

"Just like old times."

"Not exactly. Kevin won't be flinging food from his high-chair."

"It's hard to believe either of them was ever little enough to fit in a highchair. In fact, each time I come to get them they seem two years older instead of two weeks."

"I know," agreed Suzann, "I think they live to astonish me. Trisha reads as well at seven as I did when I was ten."

"I've noticed she likes to read. At a restaurant she won't return the menu until she has sounded out every word on the page. I've also noticed she tells stories. Is that progressive or regressive for a seven-year-old?"

"What kind of stories?"

"Like they have lobster for lunch every Friday and her teacher has a six-month-old baby which stays in a playpen at the back of the room."

Suzann laughed. "Your daughter thinks you never let up on the school questions. Maybe she's just trying to keep you satisfied. . . ." She paused before continuing. "But Trisha said something today that I wondered about."

"What's that?"

"She said that two weeks ago, when you took them shopping, you were trying on church clothes. She thought you might start coming to church."

"What are church clothes?" Peter seemed puzzled. "Oh. I was being fitted for a tuxedo."

"A tuxedo? What for?"

"I'm getting married again."

Had Suzann been eating, she would have choked. Had she been dancing, she would have tripped. Had she been writing, she would have scarred the page with a freak line. But just sitting—all she could do just sitting was feel the avalanche in her head and wonder if her brain was crumbling apart. And she could utter two words. "To whom?"

"Marta, of course."

48

Softly, "But Trisha said you'd stopped seeing Marta."

"What? Oh. Marta has been spending the weekends in Tucson. That's where she's from. She's making the arrangements, and her mother is sewing her wedding dress. In fact, that's kind of what I wanted to talk to you about. She'd like Trisha to be the flower girl. She already has the pattern and some material for a dress—taffeta, does that sound right? Well, we wondered if you would make it. Marta doesn't sew and you're such an excellent . . ."

"Wait a minute!" cried Suzann. "Do you know how hard it is to sew with taffeta? Do you know how little spare time I have for sewing? Did you ever think I might not rejoice at the idea of your getting remarried? I can't believe you'd do this to me. Next you'll be asking if I want to be one of the bridesmaids . . ."

"I'm sorry, Suzann." Peter rose. "Forget the dress. I'll wait for the kids in the car."

A gloom that foreshadowed the bleakness of the weekend to come was trapped inside with the slamming of the front door. *Timing. Such timing—I invite him to dinner and he asks me to sew for his wedding. Casual. So casual—my reaction is John McEnroe after a bad call on match point.*

Kevin and Trisha dashed in to grab their overnight bags. "Bye, Mom."

No hugs.

*That's fine, kids. Heap rejection on top of rejection, pour salt into the wound, fuel the anguish until it becomes inflamed. Wait a minute. Do I detect a trace of self-pity? An entire bloodstream saturated with it? Okay, Suzann. Let's hold this thing to the light and look at it from another angle. You've been clinging to a relationship afflicted with a terminal illness. Your emotions have swung like a pendulum from days that warranted hope to days that predicted despair. And the ceaseless momentum has worn thin the cord of your sanity, almost to the point of breaking. But now there will be no more dizzying pitch. It's over. You've embraced your dream for the last time. All that's left for you to do is heal.*

*Okay. So heal. Heal! I'll wait. No. I can't wait. I have to do something—put a Band-aid on my mind, swab disinfectant over my heart. Call Rose? What could Rose do? Set me up with a prince who will carry me on his white steed into happily ever after? No, I think Rose would suggest I come to the progressive dinner and look for my own prince—take my heart off "hold" and see what connections develop. But am I up to a social? Manipulating utensils? Fitting words into sentences into conversations? And what about my black veil? Will everyone recognize that I'm in mourning?*

*Cheerful. Being cheerful is essential.*

# 7

Suzann joined the troop of Forty-ninth Warders in quest of a meal, discovering one course, then moving on to the next. The progressive dinner drew a respectable crowd, but not everyone. Not Jesse and Carolyn.

Jesse had made alternate plans. The night before, after he had established himself as the Pied Piper of the piano and previous to his departure, Jesse had told Carolyn she would want to be ready by four-thirty the following afternoon.

"What for?" Carolyn had answered.

"Not 'what *for*'—'what *in*?' In jeans, a casual shirt, and tennis shoes . . . or cowboy boots. And bring a change of clothes for a nice restaurant."

"Cowboy boots? Are we going horseback riding?"

"I'm keeping the rest a surprise," said Jesse. "Just answer this. Do you want the boots with or without spurs?"

The next day, when Jesse's car pulled parallel to Carolyn's sidewalk at almost four-thirty, she was ready enough to stride out and meet him. Tyler was ready, also, and followed Carolyn to the car.

"Tyler, you can't come this time," she told him when she had detected his shadow. "You need to go back inside the house."

"I just want to say 'hi' to Jesse."

Jesse opened his door and turned to greet the little boy. "There's Tyler, my favorite four-year-old."

"Jesse, can I come with you?"

"Tyler. . . ." Carolyn had slid into the right front seat.

"I wish you could," answered Jesse, "but I've already made the plans for just two people."

"Could we leave Carolyn home?"

Jesse thought a minute. "You and Carolyn will have to decide that. *But* the one who stays here can have the big, delicious, chocolate Milky Way bar in my glove compartment."

"I'll take the candy bar," said Carolyn. "No. This isn't a time to be selfish. Tyler, you take it." She dug the Milky Way out of the glove compartment and reached across Jesse to plant it in Tyler's hand. "See you later."

Tyler looked uncertain. "But I didn't get to make a choice."

"There really never was one," Carolyn told him.

Tyler went for a new angle. "Jesse, would you make plans for three people next time?"

"One of these times, Tyler," answered Jesse. "Before long we'll all do something together."

Once they were in motion, Carolyn focused the vent's blast of cool air on her face and sank back into the seat. The new Dan Fogelberg single, one of her favorites, was wafting from the radio and she amplified the lyrics with her voice. What she really wondered about, more than whether the young man in the song would devote his life to music or law, was the details of tonight's activities. It was obvious the young man was destined to sing. She could only presume they were going to ride horses. And if so, whose? And where? And what next? The answers were not in asking; they were in waiting. When Jesse was ready to explain, she would know.

The drive was lean on conversation. A little talking, a lot of thinking. Carolyn wondered if there would be a right time tonight to tell Jesse they were getting too serious—or if there would ever be a right time.

Jesse entered the lengthy drive of a large ranch-style home on the outskirts of Scottsdale.

"Ed Cook, a man I do a lot of work with, lives here," he explained as they approached the creamy, stuccoed walls that peaked under a red tiled roof and through a hug of protective greenery.

"So this is a business call," said Carolyn. "You suggested the boots because he's from Texas and we want to win his confidence."

They crunched to a stop in the loop that bordered the house and eventually led back to the main road.

"No, he's from Wyoming. You were right yesterday when you guessed the horses. Ed mentioned he had some last week. After I showed an interest, he insisted I come ride. When I invited you, I didn't really expect it to be mystery-magazine material, but everyone needs a surprise now and then." Jesse started to get out of the car. "Oh, you can bring your extra clothes in. We'll be changing here."

They walked together up to a combination botanical garden and porch, where Jesse rang a bell that played the first stanzas of "Home on the Range." The older man who answered the door in jeans and rolled-up sleeves was not a large man—except for his smile, which made a white-planked bridge between his ears.

"Are the wrangler positions still open?" asked Jesse.

"Depends. What kind of qualifications do you have?"

"I've seen every episode of 'Bonanza' ever made."

"You're hired." Ed turned to Carolyn. "How about you?"

"Ummm. My great-grandmother knew Annie Oakley."

"That's worth a gamble. Come on in."

Jesse made introductions.

"Sorry you can't meet my wife," Ed replied. "She's visiting our daughter in Chicago."

"What does your daughter do there?" asked Carolyn.

"Studies teeth."

"She's going to dental school?"

"No. She knocks out reports for companies who make toothpaste. This might be classified information, but consumers prefer blue mint gel over green."

"I used to like the toothpaste with stripes," said Jesse. "The kind they sold when I was a kid. It was white with red stripes. If I squeezed it out carefully enough, it looked like the staff of a candy cane. And if it looked like the staff of a candy cane, it was too good to brush my teeth with, so I just licked it off. I never got a cavity in my tongue, either."

"Can you put that in writing?" asked Ed. "This might be the kind of break-through my daughter has been looking for."

They laughed.

"Hey, you didn't come here to talk with me," continued Ed. "Let me show you to the stable."

They followed Ed behind the house to a large brick building that wore the same cream stucco and tile roof as the house.

"My idea of a stable is a modest wood shack," said Carolyn. "You could sell furniture out of that place."

"That's what the horses do when they're not out giving rides," said Ed.

They entered the building, which housed two horses on one side and supplies on the other. Carolyn approached the stalls for a closer look at the huge red beasts. "I hate to be picky, but could I have the gentle one?"

"They're both gentle, honey," answered Ed. "Just show them who's the boss."

"Who is?" asked Carolyn.

"Jesse, you take care of this girl." Ed handed Jesse a bridle and carried another to a stall, where he slipped it over a horse's head. "Come on, Raisin," he cooed as he led the animal across the room to the supplies and layered him with a thin blanket and a saddle. Jesse followed with the other horse.

"Okay, Carolyn, hop up here and let me set the stirrups for you." Ed meshed his fingers into a step.

Mounted, they walked the horses across Ed's yard to a side gate that led from grass to desert. Jesse sprang down and opened it for them to pass through.

"You've ridden before, right?" he asked, climbing back into the saddle.

"Sure. When you want to go left, you stick your left arm out straight. You bend it up for right." Carolyn made the appropriate motions.

"That might get your driver's license renewed, but I don't think the horse has read the manual."

Carolyn smiled. "I've ridden a little. Dad used to take us horseback riding when we stayed in the White Mountains. But it wasn't like a roundup or anything. We'd join a line of other vacationers who followed a guide along a trail. Dad would sing cowboy songs, like 'I've Got Spurs That Jingle Jangle Jingle.' After a few summers my sisters stopped asking to go. As almost-teens, they felt that being related to someone who sang on a horse had to go in the closet with the dolls."

Carolyn was becoming accustomed to the horse's shifting back—as long as it shifted evenly. "I haven't been on a horse for a long time," she continued, "and this one seems just as big as they did when I was a little girl."

"It's possible," answered Jesse, overlooking her insecurity. "Are you ready to give these horses some exercise?"

"Before we go any faster, I'd like to get something in writing from Raisin that he won't buck me off because he was abused by a brunette as a pony, or because he doesn't like my perfume."

"You'll be okay. Just keep a firm grip on the reins."

"Aren't you afraid your horse might throw you off?"

"My grandpa had a ranch. I've been thrown off. You just have to know how to land."

"I should have brought a parachute."

"I should have brought a switch. Let's go." Jesse jabbed his heels into the sides of his horse and it leaped into a trot. Carolyn didn't have to do a thing; Raisin automatically quickened his pace to keep up with his mate.

Trotting was worse than driving a car over a succession of railroad tracks.

"How're you doing?" asked Jesse.

"I think I should have let Tyler come instead. He's the one who enjoys bouncing down the stairs seat first."

"It's smoother when you go faster. Come on." Again Jesse prodded his horse, and it shot into a lope. Carolyn kicked this time, too, and Raisin was on Jesse's tail.

Instead of hammering into her saddle, Carolyn started flowing with the new motion. There was a rhythm to loping that was as addicting as rocking on a front-porch swing. The wind that twisted her hair and cleansed her face like an astringent deceived her into believing she was flying. And Raisin was the vehicle, the extension of her powers that made riding an adventure instead of an adversary to be overcome.

They reached the crest of a hill as the sun was bringing its performance to a close. Reining their panting horses to a stop, they watched from front-row seats while colors exploded into the clouds like pastel fireworks. As the sun bowed beneath the landscape, it drew a veil of dusk across the sky that drained the colors and simulated a diamond strand of city lights on the horizon.

Even though the horses were idle, Carolyn could still feel the warm wind caressing her face. The wind, the sky, the lights, all enhanced by Jesse's presence, fused into an aesthetic climax. Carolyn had experienced other moments like this, scattered throughout the years—moments so exquisite that they redeemed life for sometimes being harsh and confusing and painful. Moments that were like a slice of happily-ever-after in a fairy tale or a visit to heaven. Moments that banished from her mind any inclination to tell Jesse their relationship was on the decline. She could put it off just one more night.

Jesse and Carolyn led the horses at an easy gait back to Ed's stable, where Jesse stripped them and returned them to their stalls. He filled their trough with fresh water and turned to Carolyn. "Hungry?"

"Starving. Are you?" They started walking to the house.

"I could eat a horse," he answered. Carolyn rebuked him with her eyes. "Just kidding."

After Ed was summoned to the back door by Jesse's three sharp raps, he gave them each access to a bathroom where they could change. When the metamorphosis was accomplished, the three walked together through the jungle-papered hall, the tomorrowland entertainment center, and the sterile living room until they were again at the front door.

"Can I fix you a drink before you go?" Ed offered, raising his brows to Carolyn.

"We don't drink," she answered.

"How do you get enough liquids?" Ed was grinning at her.

Carolyn flushed, "What I meant . . ."

"I know. I've had business lunches with Jesse. I had in mind a soda."

"We have to go," said Jesse. "I made some reservations. In fact, we need to leave in about fifteen seconds to be on schedule. But thanks. Really. We had a great time."

"We did," added Carolyn. "I got attached to Raisin. Let me know when it's his birthday and I'll send him a box of sugar cubes."

"Yeah, sure," Ed called as they were walking to Jesse's car. "I'll invite you to the party."

The entrance of the restaurant was the caboose of a retired train.

"Reservations for Mitchell," Jesse told the girl at the desk. "Jesse Mitchell." He pointed to his last name—the only one on the list accented by a star.

As they were escorted through the tables, the restaurant maintained the illusion of being a train. Even the pictures on the wall were made to look like train windows speeding by various landscapes. One picture lured Carolyn near for several moments of close inspection. It was a painting of a train window looking into the night, capturing the faint reflection of a couple finishing dessert in the dining car.

At their booth, a waitress set down two stemmed water glasses tinkling with ice, then handed Jesse and Carolyn menus backed with the same pattern of velvet ferns that garnished the wallpaper. Carolyn stroked the marbling of textures, unaware of Jesse's gaze. But a tug in her stomach reminded her the menu was to satisfy her hunger, not her fingers, and she opened the folder.

Carolyn intended to order steak—sirloin, fillet, maybe even teriyaki if the sauce wasn't too sharp. But there wasn't steak on the menu. There wasn't beef or chicken or seafood. The menu was blank except for a tiny phrase in the middle of the right-hand page. She had to bring it closer to decipher the message: "Will you marry me."

Those words by the right man could shift a woman into excitement overdrive. Unless they were presented at the wrong time. Then they could thrust her into the moment of truth. Carolyn stared at the words, as bewildered as if they had insulted her. She let them blur into a fuzzy worm and then brought them back into crisp, thin lines. Did they change? "Will you marry me." But there wasn't a question mark. Maybe she wouldn't have to answer. Wrong. Jesse was studying her. Waiting.

"It would be so easy to say yes," said Carolyn softly, without looking at him. "And it's so hard to say no."

"What does that mean?"

"It means I can't order the wedding."

They were both quiet. A waitress came and stood on the edge of their silence.

"We're not ready yet," Jesse said to the waitress.

"I'm not ready yet," Carolyn said to Jesse. "To be a wife, to have children . . . I'm not ready to be married yet."

"Sorry," said Jesse. Although it wasn't a bitter word, it lacked the sincerity of an apology. "I guess I misread the signs. I thought we were right for each other. I thought you felt the same way I did."

"You didn't misread the signs; you just overlooked one. I can't get married right now."

"Who said right now? In three months, six months even."

Carolyn closed her eyes. "You don't understand."

"I really don't."

"There's a reason I'm studying journalism instead of home economics. I want to be a journalist. I haven't wanted it for a year or three years or five years. I've wanted to write for more than half my life. Before I wrote articles for the university paper, I was editor of the high school paper. Before I was editor of the high school paper, I ran a neighborhood newspaper for eight months. Before I ran a neighborhood paper, I had written three folders full of stories. They were typed so meticulously a publisher would have to read them to know they weren't professional. My dad's secretary typed the first ones and I did the rest.

"I've always loved to write. No, I've needed to write—to define myself, to organize my emotions, to release a voice that is straining to be heard. When I write, I focus all my creativity, my mental resources, my powers of intuition on the tip of a pen. And what flows from that pen looks a lot like blue ink, but I swear it's my lifeblood. When I write well, I know the part of me I've left on the paper is the best I can give. And I can't surrender that part. I have to finish school. I have to find out if I can succeed as a journalist—if I'm professional material."

"Is there a new rule that bans married women from college?" asked Jesse.

"No. It's an old rule. Married women have babies and raise children."

Jesse handed her his menu. "Decide what you want."

"You don't have to buy me dinner."

"The dinner wasn't under the stipulation that you say yes. It can be a good-bye dinner."

Good-bye? An icy hand clutched her heart, squeezing out more words than she expected to say. "All along there have been guys who have tried to persuade me to get serious and trade my dream for theirs. And when I turned them down and we said good-bye, sometimes there was an empty space. But there was always someone else ready to step in and fill that empty space. Then you came. With a kit that contains everything that could make me love you, including a smile that hits me like a punch in the stomach and a kiss that makes me wish I were your wife. But I can't be. I'm already engaged to a typewriter. . . . They say true love conquers all, but I'm not convinced."

"Neither am I. Sometimes ambition conquers true love."

Carolyn looked away, fortifying her mind against the words.

The waitress was standing beside their booth again.

"Are you ready yet, Carolyn?" asked Jesse. "To order dinner, not get married."

If Jesse's 280ZX had been quiet as they drove to Scottsdale, starting home it was a tomb. Carolyn didn't notice where the air vent was blowing, and when Jesse clicked on the radio she didn't sing. How could she? Dan Fogelberg's new single was on, and she hated it. The streets had the eerie quality of a nightmare and the other drivers seemed as hostile as competitive racers.

When Jesse stopped in front of her house, he reached for the handle as if he were actually going to open her door or even walk her to the house.

"Don't get out," said Carolyn. Jesse moved his hand to the knee of his tan corduroys, where it softly strummed against his pants. "I better go in before I change my mind."

"Why don't you change your mind and then go in?" he asked.

Carolyn watched his fingers until they stopped moving. "I can't."

"Okay. Good luck with your career."

"You don't know how sorry I am things turned out this way," she said.

"I'm a little disappointed myself."

She looked at him one long last time, suppressing the impulse to dive into his embrace and promise to love him forever. The longer she stayed, the more keenly she felt her resolve slipping away. And yet she didn't have the power to blink. It was Jesse, who had been returning her gaze as steadily as a mirror, who suddenly turned away and broke the spell. Freed from his dark eyes, Carolyn could let herself out of the car and walk to the porch. By the time she reached the front door, he still hadn't started the engine. She paused with her hand on the knob while the wind, not the gracious wind of the early evening but a vindictive wind, taunted her through the trees. "You fool!" She flung open the door.

In her room, after she had listened to his car growl away, Carolyn didn't feel the empty space which often followed the good-bye scene of a significant romance. This time there was a cursed bottomless pit.

# 8

Suzann had been home from the progressive dinner since 9:30, almost three hours. Propped in bed, she was still holding the novel she'd picked up forty-five minutes earlier, and she'd already covered nearly three pages. For most people, placing themselves behind a book encourages reading; for Suzann, small black print was sometimes the stimulus for a wandering mind. Tonight she responded to the book by analyzing her evening.

*How absurd to think that tonight I could find the man who would bring romance back into my life. What did I expect?*

*Progressive dinner, course one: Suzann White appears in the entry hall of a house circulating with appetizer trays. Her eyes sweep the crowded living room for a familiar face. The man on whom her gaze settles would be impossible to connect with a name, for they have never met. And yet she has imagined a face such as his every time she has read romantic fiction.*

*He looks up. His gaze darts around the room like a bee picking out a flower—until it reaches Suzann, where it stops. It has to stop, because his eyes have locked into hers. For either to turn away could mean wrenching an eyeball from a socket. And suddenly, what was once the clamor of conversation and laughter becomes for them the impassioned symphony of an orchestra. What was once a room full of people becomes a garden full of statues. And as they stare into the eyes across the room, each one sees the missing piece in the puzzle of life.*

*The front door opens to admit the next cluster of guests, and as it slams behind them the spell is broken. But its effects are not forgotten. Suzann and her new contact meander among the people, stopping to smile at familiar faces, yet aware of a compulsion pushing them on to the destined confrontation. Facing each other at last, their eyes reunited, they continue their silent communion.*

*Then he speaks. "Did you come here tonight to find dinner—or true love?"*

*Suzann is startled by such boldness, but quickly regains her composure. "I came to find true love, but I won't turn down dinner."*

*They glide together from course to course, discovering one common interest after another. Suzann has never met anyone so clever, handsome, sensitive, and active in the Mormon Church. And finally, when they are sitting with only the crumbs of strawberry shortcake left on their plates, he suggests, "Let me give you a ride home."*

*Suzann considers abandoning her car at the appetizer house, but in the end confesses it is parked there. They are both momentarily disappointed. But only momentarily, because it is obvious they will be spending a lot of time together in the days to come.*

*Is that what I expected?*

In reality, the only interaction that came close occurred when she appeared in the entry hall of the second house. Her gaze scanned the living room, which needed about ten more people to be called crowded, and screeched to a stop on Wayne Cardon. She had attended his Sunday School class when she wasn't doing Relief Society business. Wayne had asked her out, four times, five times; how many times had she turned him down? Not because *he* wasn't worth her attention, but at the time she'd felt that dating wasn't. She hadn't noticed what nice, straight teeth he had when he smiled. And he was always smiling. Maybe she had overlooked Wayne's being attractive and friendly two months ago, but it was plenty obvious to her tonight.

Their eyes met. Without music, without the magic to transform people to stone, but not without acknowledgement. They did exchange smiles. *Smiles might be a little short on commitment, but they aren't without promise.* Suzann followed him across the room.

"Hello, Wayne," she said when they were within conversation radius.

"Suzann!" He looked delighted. "What are you doing here?"

"Gaining about three pounds."

He expanded his smile. "I can't remember the last time I saw you at a ward activity."

"It was March of 1872." She grinned at him. "Come on. I attend these things."

Wayne's expression said he wasn't convinced.

"Sometimes I'm working behind the scenes," she added.

"Okay," said Wayne, "so what else have you been doing besides going to ward activities?"

"Nothing much . . . holding down a full-time job, managing a home, raising a family . . ."

"Sounds like you're still busy."

Was he referring to her having blocked his every attempt to take her out? She'd gamble. "It wasn't just that I was busy; it was bad timing for me to start something a couple months ago."

They both turned to watch a girl approach from the kitchen. She was Sherri Nelson, a knockout blonde who had a clothes allowance as big as the national defense budget. Weaving her arm through Wayne's, Sherri bubbled, "I was going to make you a salad, but there are so many things to choose from. Besides lettuce and tomatoes, they have cheese and mushrooms and beans and sprouts and sunflower seeds and about five dressings. You better fix your own."

To Suzann, she smiled with her lips, but the ice in her eyes could have sunk the Titanic. Slowly releasing Wayne's arm, she started back towards the kitchen. Before he left Suzann to follow Sherri, he whispered, "*Now* is kind of bad timing for me."

It was then that Suzann took a ratio count and discovered that the women outnumbered the men four to one. Why hadn't she recognized the forces of the dating game? She'd forgotten how much fun it could be—best friend pitted against best friend, no rules, and a score card that was tallied every Friday and Saturday night. Uh-oh. Did she still have the equipment? The face, the figure, the small talk? In a game that was so comprehensive that it took into account not only appearance but talents, wit, occupation, associates, property, and net worth, one had to be prepared. Did she have the funds? This game could blow the top off a Mastercard limit in clothes alone. And for all the investment, it was still risky. There was no guarantee of being victorious or staying victorious. The dating game could last years—a lifetime. And Suzann had thought she could put all her chips on July 18 and come out the big winner.

I was crazy to think I'd find him tonight, Suzann repeated as she closed her book and set it on the nightstand. She reached for the knob to turn off the lamp, but before she could twist it her movement was arrested by an unexpected noise. She brought her arm back to the bed and listened.

*Tap tap. Scrape. Tap tap.*

Panic exploded through her body. Someone was breaking in. Suzann grabbed a fistfull of bedspread in each hand. Adrenaline was overtaking her circulation system like a tidal wave. *Wait. Maybe it's just a tree brushing against the window. No; there aren't any trees against that side of the house. Someone is breaking in.*

Suzann dashed to her bedroom door and locked it, then grabbed the phone on her nightstand. There was a sticker on the receiver listing emergency phone numbers. She disciplined her fingers to push the buttons slowly, surely.

"This is Suzann White at 1334 West Grove, number 56. Someone is breaking into my house. Can you get a policeman here right away?"

"Just a minute. I'll have to connect you to another department."

Suzann repeated her message and set down the phone.

*Tap tap. Squeak. Scrape.*

*They're not going to come soon enough. They won't be able to find me in the maze of condominiums. What can I do? I'll call Jesse. He lives close. If ever I could use a home teacher . . .*

The phone rang twice before Suzann heard a click and recognized Jesse's voice.

"Carolyn? I thought of calling you, too."

"No, this is Suzann. Jesse, someone is breaking into my house."

"Do you want me to call the police?"

"I did. I want you to come over. I'm afraid they won't get here in time; you know how hard this place is to find."

"Okay, Suzann; I'll be right there."

Suzann returned the receiver to its cradle. Maybe the trespasser had given up and gone away.

*Tap, tap.*

She said a prayer. What else was there to do? She could run downstairs to the kitchen and grab a knife, but she'd have to go past the window where the sounds were coming from. What if he broke in just before she rushed by? Suzann shuddered. Maybe she should hide somewhere, like in the shower; or yell, "Harry, someone's breaking in! Get the gun!" The easiest thing would be to scream, but that didn't seem right, either.

Suzann heard scuffling. The tapping and scraping stopped, and instead there were soft footsteps brushing against the carpet. *He's inside. He's going to get me. To kill me. This is it.* She lay paralyzed, afraid to move, afraid not to move. The stairs creaked under the weight of an ascending body. He was on the second level now. Her level.

She could hear breathing outside her door, and then she watched the doorknob jiggling and twisting. It felt as though he were wrenching something inside her, too, and she clenched her teeth to keep from crying out. Did he know someone was in here? Surely the light escaping under the door had tipped him off. He slammed his weight against the door; when it didn't open, he kicked sharply at the wood before moving on.

Thank goodness the kids were with their father. It sounded like he was in Trisha's room. What treasures he could find there! Hanging on the wall was a collection of her limited-edition watercolor designs; in the closet hung the coat Trisha called mink despite its bright blue artificial fur; and on her dresser was the Lifesaver necklace that would make any jeweler gawk. Too bad the bulldog on the bed was stuffed. Suddenly Suzann resented his being in Trisha's room so fiercely she climbed out of bed and stood up. Not that she knew what to do next, but she stood by her bed clenching her fists.

The doorbell rang. Then three powerful knocks were followed by, "Open up. Police."

Suzann had been safe behind the locked door. She hesitated to venture beyond it now. What would the policeman do if she didn't answer? The trespasser wasn't going to wait and find out. he started leaping down the stairs.

"He got in here," said a deep voice. The cops had found the window, and it sounded like one of them was climbing in.

Suzann heard the front door flung open and slammed shut. The thief was gone—purged from her home. She was safe, alive, her brush with danger only a memory. She checked her body for wounds and laughed nervously. And then cried sobs that jerked from her chest.

After her outburst, she listened again. At first she couldn't hear anything; then there were voices outside by the front door. Was that Jesse's voice?

"Suzann?" Jesse had opened the door and was calling to her. "Suzann? Are you okay?"

"I'm okay." She pulled on her robe and started down the stairs just as Jesse was bounding up. At first she thought he was going to trample over her but he stopped before they collided and clasped her shoulders between his hands.

"Are you okay?"

"I'm okay."

"Did he hurt you?"

"He didn't touch me."

Suzann could see the policemen through the open front door.

"Are you the lady that called?" one of them yelled up to her.

"Yes." Jesse was leading her down the stairs.

"We'll need to get some information from you, but we're going to take this guy down to the station and book him first. We'll get back with you tomorrow. Don't move or anything."

"No." As she approached the front door she could see a third figure on the porch, who wasn't wearing all blue and whose wrists were bound in handcuffs.

"You're lucky your boyfriend came along," said the other policeman.

"What?"

"We had just climbed in through the window that was jarred loose when we heard this guy"—he jerked the handcuffs—"shoot out the front door. We started after him but by the time we got out of the house your friend was on his tail. He's the one who tackled the crook and brought him back."

Suzann turned to Jesse. "You caught him?"

"I was coming up to your door and he practically ran into my arms. But he veered to the side when he saw me so I had to chase him."

Suzann had avoided looking directly at the trespasser, but now she felt compelled to know what kind of face belonged to a man who would invade her domain. She forced herself to look at him. He was just a boy, probably still in his teens. His hair had the appearance of having been cut and styled by a three-year-old. He wore the regulation uniform for a high school or college campus: Nikes, jeans, polo shirt. But his eyes didn't conform. They weren't eager or shy. They could have been marbles.

"We'll see you tomorrow," said one of the officers. "What's your name?"

"Suzann White."

"And this is," he glanced at a pad, "1334 West Grove?"

"Number 56."

"Okay. We'll be back to get a report."

They left Jesse and Suzann alone.

"Jesse, thanks for coming," she said.

"I'm glad I could do something."

"Do something? You were a hero."

"Did your kids sleep through the excitement?" Jesse asked.

"They're with their father."

"You were all alone? What a terrible thing to happen!"

"At least it's over now." Suzann shook her head. "I hope it never happens again."

"Maybe we should see if we can fix your window. That might reduce the chances."

They walked together to the side of the house, outside the dining room where the intruder had pried the window out of its tracks.

"I almost bought a burglar alarm once," said Suzann, "but it was a kit, and I could see myself wiring the thing so a siren would go off every time my kids opened the front door."

"I bought one," said Jesse as he inspected the window, "but before I could put it together my brother's birthday came around and I gave it to him."

"I'd need a kit *and* an electrical engineer for my birthday to come out with an alarm system."

Jesse smiled and pointed to the edge of the window. "Your intruder bent the frame. It'll fit back in—but you should have it fixed so it can't be popped right out again."

"Okay."

Jesse eased the window back into place and turned to Suzann. "Will you be all right?"

"In about two weeks my heartbeat will return to normal."

He placed his hand on her shoulder and gave her a sympathetic smile. "Can I do anything else?"

"I'm opening up a position for night watchman. You could apply."

"Would it make you feel better if I slept on your couch tonight?"

"Would you mind? There's a chance I could go back to sleep if you stayed here."

"I'll stay."

Jesse followed her into the house.

"Let me get you a pillow," said Suzann. In a minute she was back with a Mickey Mouse pillow and Winnie the Pooh sheet. She smiled as she laid them on the couch. "Sorry they don't match."

"They're both Disney; I'd say that's a match. The thing that concerns me is—do I get one bedtime story or two?"

Suzann smiled and dropped on the couch next to the pillow. "You know what bothers me? That someone could come into my house and just browse through all my possessions as if they were his for the picking. Not that I have that much to offer. I don't own a thing that could support a drug habit for more than two weeks. But you know what else? It's not the material things so much; that guy didn't even take anything, and he didn't hurt me. But the terror of it . . ." Suzann looked across the hall at the window which had become a door. "The darkness and I have never been real good friends, but I think this will put even more of a strain on our relationship."

Jesse watched her for a moment. "It's like any bad experience, Suzann. It will be hard for a while, but the intensity wears off."

In the morning, as Suzann dressed, she was planning the deluxe breakfast she would make for Jesse in payment. She knew she would fix orange frosts to drink, but she couldn't decide on her special omelettes or waffles and bacon for the main course. Maybe Jesse would be up and she could ask him.

As she came down the stairs, he was tying his shoes.

"I'm glad you're awake, because I have something very important to ask you," Suzann said, when he had looked up to acknowledge her.

"What's that?"

"Do you prefer omelettes or waffles?"

"I hope you don't mean for breakfast."

"You could eat them for lunch or dinner, I guess, but my family eats them for breakfast and we haven't experienced any dire consequences."

"I love omelettes and I love waffles. But I'm playing basketball with some guys this morning and I should have left five minutes ago."

"You expect me just to say 'Okay, thanks, and good-bye' after all you did last night?"

"I haven't had time to make a list of what I expect from you," Jesse grinned at her, "but 'Okay, thanks, and good-bye' will probably do."

"If you won't take breakfast, let me bring over your dinner one night this week."

Jesse shook his head. "You don't need to do that."

"I make some terrific lasagne."

"With ricotta cheese?"

"And fresh spices."

"How soon can you have it over?"

"Is Wednesday night okay?"

Jesse stood up and started to the door, "Fine. I'll set out the checkered tablecloth for Wednesday."

She nodded and waved good-bye. Bringing dinner to Jesse wasn't invading Carolyn's territory, was it? Suzann needed to think. She picked up her novel . . .

# 9

The car smelled as though it were running on tomato sauce instead of gas.

"Why don't *we* get lasagne tonight?" asked Kevin. He was holding a basket of garlic bread and lifted up a corner of the foil covering to break off a piece of crust.

"I told you. Our batch burned and this goes to Jesse."

"Why are you taking Jesse dinner?" Trisha asked. She was holding a bowl of green salad and had no desire to sneak out a piece of lettuce. "You've never made dinner for Jesse before."

"Jesse helped me when you were with your father last weekend."

"What did he do?" asked Trisha.

"Just helped with some things. He helped fix a window." Suzann pulled in front of Jesse's townhouse. "Don't get out yet. Let me help you with the food. This dinner was too much work to dump on the sidewalk."

Suzann assisted the children out of the car and then lifted the lasagne from the back with hot pads. They made a procession to Jesse's front door. Suzann was juggling for a free hand with which to ring the bell when Jesse opened the door.

"Mmmm," said Jesse. "Looks like you need a kitchen. Follow me."

"This is a change, us coming to your house, isn't it, Jesse?" said Kevin.

"I think it's a change for the better," answered Jesse as he took the bread from Kevin and set it on the counter.

"There you go." Suzann placed the steaming casserole next to the garlic bread. "Let me know if you think I should open up an Italian restaurant."

Jesse smiled. "You're going to stay and eat it with me, aren't you?"

"No. You can freeze what's left over and have it another time."

"Oh, come on," said Jesse, "There's so much here, I bet the four of us couldn't finish it."

"I'll stay," replied Trisha.

"I'll stay, too," said Kevin. "Lasagne is my favorite and when Mom was . . ."

"If my kids are going to eat here," interrupted Suzann, "Maybe I'd better stay, too. If you're sure it's okay."

"I insist." Jesse lifted some plates from the cupboard and Suzann located the silverware drawer, enlisting Trisha to help her set some on the table.

"Instant family," said Jesse, after they had sat down and blessed the food. He spooned a block of lasagne onto his plate and passed it on. "Who did anything exciting today?"

"I did," said Trisha. "I rode a bike without training wheels."

"That's great," replied Jesse.

"Something exciting happened to me, too," said Kevin.

"What?"

Kevin thought a few seconds. "What exciting thing happened to me, Mom?"

They laughed.

"I know something," said Suzann. "Didn't you go swimming today and jump off the diving board?"

"I did." Kevin brought two fingers representing legs in front of him and used them to illustrate his narration. "I jumped way into the air"—his fingers flew up—"and then landed—splash—into the water!" His fingers plopped into the lasagne.

"Kevin," Suzann sighed, "wipe off your fingers."

"I'll wipe them off with my tongue." Kevin sucked the lasagne off in his mouth.

"Sorry," Suzann apologized. "This is the first time anything like this has ever happened."

Jesse smiled.

"But, what about when . . ." started Trisha.

"Trisha, you know our table manners are impeccable," Suzann cut in. She turned to Kevin. "If you mistake your fingers for your fork one more time you'll have to wait for us in the car."

"Terrific lasagne," said Jesse.

When four plates showed only scant remains of an Italian dinner, Trisha turned to the window which had been competing with the lasagne for her attention all through the meal. "Can I be excused?" she asked.

"Excused to where?" answered Suzann.

"If I put my plate on the counter, can I go next door? I saw some kids out the window who have a puppy."

"Okay."

"Me, too?" asked Kevin.

"Yes. You, too."

The children were up with their plates and out the door. Suzann leaned back into the thick padding of her chair and released a cross between a smile and a sigh.

"Great lasagne," repeated Jesse.

"Thanks."

"Did you get your window fixed?" Jesse took another piece of garlic bread.

"Yes. The policemen came back, too, for a report, and they said I needed to press charges for breaking and entering."

"Did they say anything about giving me a medal?" Jesse was smiling.

"No. But they were both wearing big gold medals that said 'Captured Suzann's burglar.' "

He laughed.

"How was your basketball game Saturday morning?" she asked.

"Close," answered Jesse. "We had to go into overtime. Did you ever decide between the omelette or waffle?"

"No. I didn't have to decide because the cook took the morning off."

Jesse smiled and Suzann basked in the warmth of his gaze.

Only when she realized she was enjoying his attention did she feel uncomfortable and turn away. This man was practically married to one of her good friends.

"What do you do when you're not working, Suzann?"

"It seems like I'm always working. No, wait, there have been moments . . . I like to read and listen to music and go shopping and jog and do things with the kids. We flew a kite the other evening and I forgot how much fun it could be. What do you do when you're not working?"

"I like sports—playing, watching, reading about them in the paper. And music. And sometimes I'll get in the mood to whip something up in the kitchen."

"Really? Do you have a specialty?"

"It changes. Right now I'm perfecting my sweet and sour pork."

"When you have it perfected, would you mind passing on the recipe?"

"I couldn't."

"Top secret?"

"No. I measure by taste and texture, not cups and spoons."

"Oh. Well, I think it is nice you know how to cook."

"When you aren't married and get tired of going out to eat, you don't have a lot of other options."

"I've been thinking maybe that would change—your not being married, I mean. You and Carolyn seem pretty serious."

For a minute he just looked at her, then he smiled and picked up his fork, twisting it in his fingers. "I thought we were serious, too. But she's more serious about journalism. Carolyn and I played our good-bye scene Friday night."

"Oh," said Suzann. She usually won high scores in compassion, but tonight she had to struggle to commiserate. It was strange, too, because she'd always liked Jesse. But maybe it wasn't strange. Maybe she liked Jesse more than she had realized. Suzann felt guilty for lacking sufficient sympathy and for bringing up the subject. "Sorry."

"Me, too. I think I would have picked major surgery before this."

"I know," said Suzann, and she did, but there was a twinkle in her eye when she added, "It's like any bad experience, Jesse. It will—wait a minute—be hard for a while, but the intensity wears off."

Jesse smiled. "Did you have permission to quote me?"

"You recognized it," she said.

"Jesse's consoling remark to Suzann who had just been terrorized by a burglar. Only why doesn't it sound so consoling?"

"I guess it takes someone with a great deal of patience to feel wonderful because time heals all wounds." Suzann stood up with her plate. "Shall we do the dishes?"

As they cleared the table, Suzann was aware of Jesse's presence in a way she had never been before when they passed or worked close to each other. Hands that normally cleared leftovers from a dish in two or three swipes with a spatula were using four and five strokes. When their eyes caught, she responded with a smile which she thought she had tucked away inside her high-school yearbook.

Trisha and Kevin bounded back into the kitchen when the cleanup was practically finished.

"Can we have a puppy, Mom?" asked Trisha.

"Trisha, we're gone all day long. Even a hamster would get bored at our house."

"Jesse, do you have any toys?" asked Kevin.

"So they tell me. But I don't think they're the kind you have in mind."

"What kind are they?"

"A video recorder, stereo, camera equipment, computers."

"Yeah. Those will do."

"Kevin, we need to go," said Suzann. "Jesse probably has other things to do."

"Actually, I did have something else planned tonight, but I need some help with it."

"What?" came a chorus from the Whites.

"It's my mom's birthday on Sunday. She lives in Lakeside and I'm sending her a tape. I need a chorus to help me with 'Happy Birthday.' "

"We aren't exactly the Von Trapps," said Suzann.

"Who were the Von Trapps?" asked Trisha.

"Wonderful singers."

"Mom! We are *too* wonderful."

"I knew it," said Jesse. "No one escape into Switzerland; I'm getting my tape recorder."

"Switzerland?" whispered Trisha when Jesse had left. "That's where Mark's brother went on a mission. Do you think Jesse knows what he's talking about?"

"Yes. It has to do with the Von Trapps."

After they had recorded the traditional birthday song for his mother, Jesse played it back and told Trisha, "You were right," but as he continued, "You're wonderful," he was looking at Suzann.

It was after nine when Jesse walked the Whites to their car. He helped Trisha and Kevin inside and turned to their mother. "I'd like to see you again, Suzann," he said, "but I have to warn you. I'm on the rebound from another relationship."

"I'd be willing to overlook that if you would."


When Suzann heard the doorbell ring at 5:35 on Friday afternoon, intuition told her it was a water-softener salesman. Actually, it was Jesse, but holding a box in one hand and a tool kit in the other, he could have been a water-softener salesman.

"I've come to install your burglar alarm," he said.

"You have?" Her smile was undiluted delight. She couldn't decide whether it was the added security of an alarm system or seeing Jesse again that made her so happy.

While Jesse untangled wires and fished them down the walls through the attic, Suzann made tacos, and Trisha and Kevin drew pictures. Had they been racing, Suzann's dinner would have finished first in thirty minutes. The pictures took forty-five and would have come in next, followed by the alarm system, which Jesse completed in two and a half hours. It would have taken longer had he responded to Suzann's pleas to stop and eat dinner, but he saved that for afterwards.

"Good tacos," said Jesse.

"They're even better when they haven't been sitting all night."

"Oh, and I was stalling because I thought they had to age, like wine."

A crash exploded in the corner. Kevin had sneaked one of Jesse's screwdrivers from his tool kit and disassembled the tray that held the microwave oven.

"Kevin, go to your room. Do not pass go. Do not collect $200," scolded Suzann. She flew across the kitchen to inspect the damages and repair the tray, leaving Jesse at the table with Trisha.

"I don't understand about passing go and the $200, either," whispered Trisha, "but sometimes she says it."

"Oh, but I understand," Jesse answered. "It has to do with a game called 'Monopoly.' "

"Monopoly? I know Monopoly. When my mom and dad used to be married, sometimes they had friends over, and they would get out that game. I would play with the little pieces they weren't using, like the iron and the thimble and the dog and the hat. I'd sit by Mom and she'd point to a row of bright red houses and say, 'We're waiting for someone to land on those hotels.' " Trisha stopped and looked at her mother, who almost had the tray back in its original position. "Sometimes I think she's still waiting. Oh, not for someone to land on her hotels. Just for . . . I don't know."

Suzann returned to the table. "I hope you don't come over here to relax," she told Jesse.

"Of course not. I can relax at home."

When her children had been coerced to bed, Suzann and Jesse played Boggle, a word game, at the kitchen table. After several rounds, they didn't need to add up the score to determine that Suzann had smeared Jesse.

"When we play basketball, I'll let you win," she said.

"You think I have one of those complexes about having to win? I don't have one of those complexes." Jesse picked up the game box which contained all the letter-covered cubes. "Let me put this away for you." He tossed the Boggle game into the garbage.

Suzann laughed. "Remind me never to let you put away my silverware."

"Remind me," said Jesse, "that when you say, 'I warn you, I've played quite a bit,' you actually mean, 'I'm the undisputed world champ.' "

"Word games I'm good at. If I played life as well as I play Boggle, then . . ." she stopped.

"What?"

"Maybe I wouldn't be in the singles ward."

Jesse looked into her delicate gray eyes. "Tell me about your marriage, Suzann."

And she told him about Peter, about how he had proposed to her at the top of the double ferris wheel, how he hired a band to play "Happy Birthday" on the porch for her one year, how he took colored slides in the delivery room when her children were born, and how he made Mickey Mouse pancakes on Saturday mornings. She told him how he brushed her hair at night and carved "I love you" messages in the soap, and rocked with her in his arms, and left her for a woman at work.

"The other night," she said, "when you told me you were on the rebound from another relationship, I forgot to tell you I've been on the rebound for two years."

Jesse took her hand. "It's a good thing we can bounce."


The next time Jesse and Suzann spent the evening together, it was on a real date. First they went to an interesting restaurant, the kind that has such curious things all over the wall that it's easy to forget about the menu. There was a salad bar that offered practically every fruit and vegetable currently available in the Southwest, and dinner selections that challenged the experimental diner and satisfied the traditional.

After a meal that was worth every calorie, Jesse took Suzann to the Neil Diamond concert, using tickets which had cost a friend six hours of standing in line for the privilege of purchasing.

Music did something to Suzann. It always had. When she was eleven, her older brother had started a band. As she heard one of his friends singing into the microphone, it gave her the chills. She thought she was in love. Tonight, hearing Neil Diamond gave Suzann the chills and made her think she was in love, too. With Neil Diamond or Jesse? She didn't know. All she knew was that she never wanted it to end.

When Jesse brought her home, he lifted her face and kissed her so softly she thought she was going to melt into the night. Later, after he had gone and before she had fallen asleep, she decided if she had been Carolyn, she would never have picked journalism.

# 10

For Carolyn, the days that followed her last encounter with Jesse were splattered with moments in which she regretted picking journalism, too. Even writing didn't shove Jesse out of her mind. As she was trying to finish the final paper of one of her summer-school classes, she realized that, although there had been more time to write since she had stopped seeing Jesse, she had accomplished less. It was harder to concentrate.

Carolyn dropped her pen. She shoved the stack of papers away from her, within an inch of falling to the floor. *I need a break,* she sighed.

Carolyn dug into her purse for a candy bar. There was nothing like a little chocolate to revive the spirits. She sensed the crackle of a paper wrapping and drew a Milky Way from the gaping jaws of brown leather. A Milky Way. Jesse had used a Milky Way bar as the consolation prize for Tyler when he couldn't join them on their last date. The mystery date. She had assessed the clues right when she had suspected horseback riding. She remembered the unexpected elation of galloping on a horse. She remembered the wind which had accompanied the night like a soft musical theme, and the brilliant explosion of colors when the sun had dropped from the sky. But it was being with Jesse which had fused the various delightful elements into real magic. It was being with Jesse that made horseback riding in Scottsdale an experience not likely to be equalled. Carolyn stuck the unopened Milky Way back into her purse. Funny how a little bar of chocolate could dampen the spirits.

Maybe a movie would give her mind the needed vacation. She found the paper in the family room and the movies in section B. Jesse had taken her to all the good adventure shows, which drastically reduced the selection. Carolyn suspected a romance would do more harm than good and she wasn't roused by any of the documentaries. Her mind would have to forego the theater for another vacation spot.

Like the mall. What woman could have a bad day when she found the shoes that would set off that dress in the closet, or the unusual blouse that would be at the crest of fashion in three weeks? But when Carolyn thought of looking dazzling without finding the seal of approval in Jesse's eyes, she put her checkbook away without bothering to add up the balance.

Now that candy, movies, and shopping had been scratched off, the list of life's great pleasures was dwindling. There had to be something that memories of Jesse wouldn't spoil. But maybe suppressing thoughts of Jesse wasn't the answer; maybe opening up about what had happened would help. Talking with Alice could be like a session with an analyst. Carolyn phoned her sister.

Alice's two oldest children, Tyler and Janice, could have both aced a test in telephone courtesy. Unless, of course, they tried to answer the same call, which happened 95 percent of the time Carolyn called. Like today. Instead of the "Hello. Madsen residence. Tyler (or Janice) speaking," which either child was capable of rendering, Carolyn had to pull away from Janice's shrill, "I want to! I want to!" and Tyler's "It's my turn! Let me have it!" Knowing that the louder they cried, the sooner Alice would intercept the phone, Carolyn held the receiver at arm's length until she recognized her sister's voice.

"Sorry," Alice began by apologizing.

"That's okay. If I called and didn't get World War III, I'd be afraid I had the wrong number."

"We stage those fights to discourage phone solicitors."

"Does it work?"

"That depends. What do you want?"

"Do you have a minute to talk?"

"Sure, Carolyn, but hold on and let me get some mending."

"I meant in person. By the time I get there you'll have fifteen minutes to find a needle and some thread."

"I don't mend person-to-person. If it's that important, I'll give you the undivided attention only a mother taking care of four small children is capable of."

Carolyn hit every traffic light green and was at her sister's house in fourteen minutes. She hesitated before ringing the bell. She couldn't remember if the kids fought over answering the front door, too, so she knocked and let herself in. "Alice?"

"I'm in the family room, Carolyn, nursing the baby. Come on back."

Carolyn walked through a tract home with every upgraded feature and found her sister on the couch. Tyler, Janice, and Josh, who had spent the week before at her house, swarmed over her the minute she sat down. Seeing them reminded her of the life that had gone from their home when the children had left. In the wake of tranquility, she had almost forgotten to notice it.

She gave them each a hug. "What do you think about your new baby? Does he cry a lot? Can he say your names yet?

"Timothy doesn't cry," said Tyler.

"And he doesn't say our names," added Janice.

Alice had buttoned her blouse and was patting the baby on her shoulder. "I requested a quiet model."

Timothy erupted with a burp that resembled a sonic boom.

"But I settled for a good eater," continued Alice. She turned to Tyler. "Why don't you take the kids in your room and draw some pictures for Carolyn? I bet she'd really be happy if you made her some pictures to take home."

"Okay. C'mon, Janice. C'mon, Josh." Tyler jumped down and started towards the hall.

"C'mon Josh," said Janice after she fell in line behind Tyler.

"I figured you didn't come here to tell me you're engaged." Alice was slowly swaying with Timothy.

"How do you know that?"

"Because you said you wanted to talk, not 'I have something to tell you.' "

"Astute, Alice. I'm not engaged . . . but I had the chance to be last weekend."

Alice winced. "You turned Jesse down?"

"I had to. I have two more years of school to complete. I can't worry about taking on a husband and starting a family."

"He proposed and you said no?"

"I'm going to be a journalist, remember?"

"But Jesse is so handsome. And clever. And easy to talk to. And fun to be with . . ."

"Alice, I said no."

"You could have at least married him for his money."

They laughed.

"Sometimes I'm sorry I said no," said Carolyn.

"You feel you might have made a mistake?"

"Yes, sometimes. So tell me what a life of drudgery it is to be a homemaker."

Alice smiled and kissed Timothy's soft pink forehead before she put him down in her lap. "You caught me on the wrong day. Everything has gone right so far. I didn't wash any Kleenexes with the laundry, our favorite casserole is in the oven and will be ready for dinner, and Tyler and Janice have only fought once today."

"Over the phone."

"Oh. Make that two fights. They both wanted to bring me a diaper for Timothy, too. But no one lost any blood. And at least when there was trouble, it was because they were both so eager to help. And then all four kids took a nap at the same time, so I could do whatever I wanted."

"What did you do?"

"I slept, too."

"Oh."

"And I wasn't awakened by a phone solicitor."

"You screen those by the fighting kids, remember?"

"But the kids were asleep too, remember?" said Alice. "It's been a good day. Oh. This isn't what you want to hear, is it?"

"Maybe it is. If no Kleenexes in the wash and a nap are all it takes to bring a homemaker ecstasy, I think I've made the right decision."

Alice grinned. "I've oversimplified. It's not just smoothly performed actions that gives me satisfaction. When a home is run with love and order and fun, it takes on an atmosphere that is actually sublime. And to have a part of that atmosphere, to give to it and take from it, is a privilege. It's not the list of mundane chores or duties, it's the feeling—like you're creating something greater than any of its parts—something awesome, beautiful, eternal."

"I admire you for feeling that way. But I don't know if I could. And you know what scares me? I don't know if I want to."

Alice stroked Timothy's fine, downy scalp. "Don't judge by tending my kids last week. It's different with your own. You love them so much, they're worth slaving over a little." Alice was fingering Timothy's tiny hands now. "But I thought it was different between you and Jesse. I thought he transcended your other boyfriends—the ones you exchanged like library books. After watching you with Jesse, I can't believe you turned him down."

"But I've wanted to be a journalist so much longer than I've wanted Jesse Mitchell. I'm afraid if I gave that up, I'd always regret it."

"You don't regret giving up Jesse?"

"Wait a minute. You're supposed to be consoling me. I already feel bad about breaking up with Jesse. Don't rub it in."

"I'm sorry. You'll be very happy being a journalist. I think you did the right thing."

"Now I feel much better. Thanks."

"Wait. Give me one more chance. I know you've always loved to write. And you're good. Carolyn, you're really good. When you were sixteen you were writing things that could make me cry. At seventeen, you were writing things that could alter my opinion. If you didn't use that talent, it would be wrong."

Carolyn sighed. "That's more like it."

Tyler danced back into the family room flapping papers, followed by Janice and Josh doing the same dance.

"We drew you some pictures," Tyler sang. "I made one of a dwarf for Jesse. And when you give it to him, remind him about the three of us doing something together, okay? Like he promised."

"Tyler, Jesse and I aren't seeing each other any more. We broke up."

Tyler's expression turned bleak. "Does that mean I have to break up with him, too?"

"No. You don't have to break up with him, too. But you'll have to find another rendezvous point besides my house."

Tyler faced Alice. "Mom, I'm afraid I won't get to see Jesse anymore, and that makes me sad." He was fighting tears.

Alice turned to Carolyn. Her face was as sad as Tyler's, but she wasn't doing as well with the tears. One slipped down her cheek.

"I think I'd better go," said Carolyn. "I need to finish a paper I'm working on."

"And have the neighbors think we tortured you? No. We can do a better job of cheering you up than this. Oh, I have something I was going to show you."

Alice spread Timothy's blanket on the floor and laid him on it. Then she dug through a stack of video recorder tapes until she pulled one from the pile. "This is Robin Williams's imitation of Elmer Fudd singing 'Fire,' only he sings it 'Fiwer.' You'll love it. You can watch it while I'm finding something else for you."

Alice started the tape and left the room. Even Carolyn had to laugh as she watched the performance. When it was through, Alice was back with a leather notebook. "My journal," she said as she thrust it into Carolyn's hands. "Read December thirteenth."

December 13. When I step out of bed in the morning, I feel as if I'm stepping off the Rotor — that amusement park ride like a big drum. It spins around so fast that gravity plasters you to the side. Even when the floor drops, you remain on the wall, held in place by the motion. Nothing nauseates me like the Rotor. And morning sickness.

I hoisted myself out of bed, showered, and made breakfast with my head spinning. As Alex was leaving for work, I was tempted to wrap myself around his leg and plead, "Can I come, too?"

I restrained myself and sorted laundry. Three piles of clothes, like colorful haystacks, still loom in my family room. I'm afraid they will be looming for a long time. The washer is on strike. Three loads a day, four days a week— only a mother could perform under such a demanding schedule.

Tyler found my stash of peanut butter cups while he was playing Mr. Pest Control in the cupboards with the spray bottle. I had four peanut butter cups. They were going to last me through the week. I estimate they lasted Tyler six minutes. I couldn't even find the wrappers to lick the chocolate off.

As I was making enchiladas, I told the children about *The Thousand and One Nights* and the girl who enthralled the Arabian king with stories night after night until he made her his wife. The plot sounded very familiar. I realized it was because I enthrall the children with stories night after night so they will let me make dinner.

I feel that the afternoons are stretching into one long afternoon, with me on the couch telling stories, leading fingerplays, and dividing my attention among the three kids who are constantly jockeying for position on my lap. Sometimes the children seem like weighted chains, wrapped around my limbs, pulling me away as I struggle for a breath of the outside world, dragging me down into an ocean of repetition and stagnation.

Suddenly I wish I were writing somebody else's life story—a day in the life of a ballerina or stewardess or even a telephone operator. My life lacks excitement. Yet I can't run away. I have some personalized stationery coming in the mail. Besides, this stage might be a little exasperating, but I give it 25 years at the most.

Carolyn looked up. "Alice, *you* should be a writer."

"No. A mother."

"After December thirteenth you still say 'a mother'?"

"I could show you other days that paint a different picture. It's easier to convey the frustration than explain the joy. Most of the time I really am happy. Being a writer couldn't be as fulfilling as being a mother."

"For you."

"Of course."

Carolyn handed Alice back her journal. "Now I really have to go. But I'll grin as I'm walking to my car so the neighbors will know I had a wonderful time."

Carolyn was sitting at her desk again. While passing through the kitchen, she had picked up a brownie, and now she nibbled on a corner of it. She pulled the stack of papers in front of her and straightened them before starting to read the essay entitled "Taking a Stand on Controversial Issues," which ran short of a conclusion.

"Gun control limits violence." "Gun control limits violence to those who can obtain guns." "There's no justice. Men are a product of their environment. Is it fair to try a man by our system when his survival has been based on a different code of laws? Penitentiaries don't reform criminals, they reinforce criminals." "There is no justice. The court system is a revolving door, spinning criminals back onto the streets. Why don't they give the murderer a medal and save the taxpayer some money in court expenses?" "Enough is enough. Nuclear nightmares threaten the globe. How much ammunition do we have to amass? How many times must we be able to blow up the earth? How many billions of dollars do we need to steal from programs which enhance life instead of destroy it?" "A nuclear freeze would be great. For the Soviets. It would be difficult to monitor compliance with such a restriction, but you can bet congressional watchdogs, Pentagon whistle-blowers, and investigative reporters would make sure that our side adhered to the limitations. What internal policing system would the almighty Kremlin have to deal with should it choose to defy the ban?"

Opinions. They can be persuasive, ridiculous, valid, or illogical, but eventually we have to adopt our own. Sometimes, because we might be confused or uninformed or preoccupied, the opinions that gel are so weak we would hesitate to express them before a mirror. But what we have to say is significant. Because today's issues are significant, and will affect life on this planet for us and all who follow. And because the side with the loudest cry will prevail, we want to mingle our voice with the chorus that speaks with the greatest wisdom, insight, and understanding.

Carolyn read on as the paper revealed the outcome of a study on how people determine their convictions. Next came the steps that she suggested to guide someone in evaluating controversial issues. She wrote about exposure, research, and reliability of sources, and mentioned a written tally sheet with a side for pros and cons. She stressed the necessity of keeping an open mind and being receptive to new ideas. Then the paper stopped. She was looking for one more idea, a point she had missed. What else was there? What else? Now that her brownie was gone, Carolyn started chewing on the end of her pen. Her brain was arching away from the pressure to generate more ideas. She was tempted to change her mind and tag an ending to what she already had. *Wait. Change your mind. That's it. As new information comes in and you reassess the situation, you must allow yourself the freedom to switch your alliance, to change your mind.*

Carolyn worked through another paragraph and concluded with a summary. "Controversy. It's inevitable. But the response you take isn't. You can determine your stand on the rock of your own conscience: research, reason, and retain the right to change your position."

She read the paper again. It still needed one more thing: to be endorsed with an 'A' by her professor.

Carolyn was surprised a week later when her instructor suggested she meet him in his office.

"I was impressed with your essay," he said, as he swivelled his chair around to face her and adjusted his glasses.

"Thank you."

"There were some weak areas." He lifted her paper from a desk covered with papers. "I marked those in red."

Carolyn nodded.

"But I think if you're willing to give it all you've got, there could be a career for you in writing."

Carolyn smiled. *I've turned down Jesse Mitchell,* she thought. *Believe me, that's giving it all I've got.*

"Well, I just wanted you to know I think you have potential, and if I can do anything to help, let me know."

"I will. Thanks. I appreciate it."

He nodded before turning back to his papers; Carolyn took the cue to retreat. As she was walking down the hall away from the office, she felt the surging satisfaction that accompanies a victory. And yet, even after such a boost of encouragement, she felt the absence of Jesse infiltrating her triumph. Surely Jesse must feel this loneliness, too.

# 11

It was several evenings later, and Carolyn was searching for her volleyball. She had expected it to be in the storage room; not finding it there, she wondered where else to look. But mostly she wondered if she would see Jesse tonight, and she wondered if they would talk.

The Forty-ninth Ward was meeting at the building to make pizzas and play volleyball—or, for those who preferred less physical aggression, video games. They had rounded up practically a truckload of Ataris, Coleco Visions, Activisions, Intellivisions, and Odysseys, plus a huge box of cartridges. Expecting volleyball to be popular also, they were setting up two nets so that four teams could be competing at once; that's why they needed Carolyn's volleyball as well as the one that belonged to the ward.

Carolyn was looking in the hall closet now. Even if she couldn't find the ball, she wouldn't be coming to the party empty-handed. Suzann, who was in charge of the pizzas, had called almost a week ago with a dough recipe for Carolyn to mix together. She had told Carolyn, "Be sure to make it in the early afternoon so it will have plenty of time to rise."

"I'll make a note. Can I do anything else?"

"Just let the dough rise a good three hours; that's all I ask."

"Okay." Then Carolyn remembered something about Suzann. "Rose told me that Peter's getting remarried. I'm sorry."

"Thanks."

"Is it going to be hard on you?"

"I don't know. I thought it was. But maybe Peter isn't right for me."

"He was never interested in the Church, was he?" asked Carolyn.

"No."

"You need to start dating again. You'll find someone who can take you to the temple, and maybe you'll see that everything was for the best. So stop turning down dates, okay?"

Suzann hesitated.

"Okay?" Carolyn persisted.

"Okay." So soft. Without conviction. Some people had to be pushed.

Carolyn closed the closet door. No volleyball. Well, she had looked. She changed her blouse, brushed a sheen of luster into her hair, and flashed on some mascara and lipstick. Reflection? Fine. From the kitchen she picked up the large bowl bursting with swollen dough and started out the back door. There it was. In the corner of the garage was her volleyball. Of course; Tyler had played with it a couple of weeks ago while she was vacuuming her car. She grabbed the ball and drove to the church.

The kitchen was where the action was. It was crowded with people rolling out dough, grating cheese, stirring sauce, and chopping vegetables, but mostly standing around. Carolyn set her bowl on the counter and stood back to watch. She had spotted Jesse grating cheese the moment she had come through the door.

"More dough," Rose acknowledged Carolyn. "Come and roll out some rectangles for these empty cookie sheets."

"Rectangles? How am I going to spin a rectangle on my finger?"

Jesse recognized her voice and turned around. They were staring at each other, masked eyes searching masked eyes. Jesse smiled and went back to the cheese. *It still hurts*, Carolyn thought. She had assumed that just being near him would make things better, but being near him wasn't enough.

A production line started to crank into action. Rectangles of dough were stretched and pressed into pans that had been greased and sprinkled with cornmeal. Suzann at the range ladled rich, red sauce over the dough, followed by Jesse's blanket of mozzarella cheese. From there the pizzas were turned over to individuals who topped them with their favorite combinations of ingredients. The first pizzas were now in the oven.

Twenty minutes later, Carolyn was still rolling dough, occasionally interrupting her assignment with glances at Jesse. It was during one of these glances that she saw Suzann lean over to check the cheese. She put her hand on Jesse's back. Suzann put her hand on Jesse's back and left it for several seconds. It startled Carolyn, like watching somebody stick a candy bar in his pocket without paying for it. *Why would Suzann do that?* Carolyn puzzled over it as she squeezed a new glob of dough with the rolling pin.

"Any more olives?" asked someone who was as concerned about the design he was making as the ingredients he was making it with. He had a border of green peppers and three diamonds of mushrooms so far.

"Did we open all the olives?" Suzann asked Jesse. "I know we bought four cans because you were rolling them to me down the aisle, trying to keep them on the brown stripe."

"I think we left a bag of things in the trunk," answered Jesse. "I'll go check."

Carolyn watched him go out the door. What was that all about? Why would Suzann and Jesse do the shopping together? Jesse wasn't on the food committee.

Rose handed Carolyn a piece of pizza on a paper plate. "To keep up your energy," she said. Rose handed pieces to Suzann and to some of the others working in the kitchen.

Carolyn's eyes followed Jesse when he came back inside with a brown paper bag and set two cans of olives by the other ingredients. Then he returned to the cheese. Suzann approached him with her pizza and he took a bite.

*They're seeing each other,* gasped Carolyn. It had only been three weeks since Jesse had proposed to her and he was already involved with someone else. Carolyn set down her pizza. It was delicious and she had been hungry, but she didn't feel like eating anymore.

As she watched them, she felt as though someone were drawing a rope tightly around her chest. *I'm jealous*, thought Carolyn. *Like a kid who wants something more because someone else has it. But I didn't know it would be so hard seeing Jesse with someone else. Yet what could I have done? Stall for four years?*

A friend of Carolyn's passed through the kitchen. "Come have some pizza with us, Carolyn."

The need for dough rectangles was diminishing, so she followed Ann Barlow to the tables in the next room. She finished her original piece without relish and wondered if it was worth eating another. She was holding her second piece when Jesse and Suzann came in and sat down together. *I'm not going to notice*, Carolyn told herself. She looked across the table. "How do you like your job, Ann?"

After dinner, after cleanup, the volleyball nets started to spread across the cultural hall. Carolyn made a trip to her car and came back bouncing the ball on her wrist.

"Oh good, Carolyn remembered to bring her ball," someone called.

"Way to go!"

"All right, Carolyn!" Bill Harris patted her on the back.

"Wait a minute. Before you pin on a medal, I have a confession to make. It's flat."

"How could you do this to us?"

"I just discovered it," she answered.

"Who else has a volleyball?"

It was a minute before Jesse replied, "I have a pump in my car."

"Go get some air," said Bill. He nudged her towards Jesse and she followed him outside. How strange it felt walking with Jesse again. Bittersweet. She didn't know whether to be solemn or ecstatic. *Be yourself.*

"How's business?" she asked.

"Great."

"How's your baseball team, the Cubs?"

"They're doing okay."

"How's your love life?" That popped out.

Jesse turned until his dark eyes were fastened on Carolyn. He laughed and then smiled at her, a smile just like the old smiles, and it made her jump inside.

"Come on, Carolyn; don't skirt the issue."

"Oh. Sorry. Did you get your home teaching done this month?" She said it before she remembered Suzann was on his beat.

Jesse stopped pulling the pump out of the trunk to give her a funny look. "Sure."

She held the ball while Jesse pumped it with air. They were so close. *This might be the closest we'll ever be again.* Carolyn blocked out the thought the moment it registered.

"Is it the way you want it now?" asked Jesse.

"No. What?"

"The ball. Is the ball the way you want it?"

"Oh." Carolyn put pressure on the leather. "The ball's fine."

Jesse returned the pump to his trunk and they started walking back to the building.

"You don't need to answer about your love life," said Carolyn. "I figured out you've got it rolling again."

"You'll make a great investigative reporter," he answered, without looking at her.


Standing in formation behind the net reminded Carolyn of the three years she had played high school volleyball. It reminded her of laps around the gym and Buster Bars for unbroken serves and Edna Johnson's ultra-short hair in pigtails and Wayne Ellington. Wayne was tall and good-looking and shy, and showed up to nearly every varsity volleyball game during Carolyn's senior year. No one was quite sure what to credit for their devoted fan, but most of them found his presence extremely motivating. Carolyn assumed he just liked watching volleyball. Then she had him in her free enterprise class the next semester. They became friends and he confessed that it was Carolyn he had liked to watch. By then, though, Wayne was dating the student body president. Carolyn had missed her chance.

The ball punched into the net and Carolyn was on her knees, bumping it up, saving the shot for someone else to knock over the net. Carolyn was not conscious of playing good ball. After years of training, it came naturally. From the way she could drive an overhead serve across the net to the way she dived for a save, from her bumps that lobbed straight and high to the setter to her spikes that slammed down into the opposite court, Carolyn proved that she had not lost her skill. And tonight, of all her outstanding moves, one pleased her more than any other. She had jumped up at the net to screen a shot at the same time that mighty Marty Evans had lunged forward to block the same shot. They slammed into each other, and Carolyn slithered to the ground. She was down for several seconds before she lifted her head. The first eyes she saw were those of Jesse, who was playing on the next court. And his eyes were saturated with concern.

Carolyn had reeled back and forth for a few moments after being helped to her feet, but the dizziness eventually subsided and she continued with her team for almost another hour and a half until the cry of "one more game" was met with overwhelming resistance. The court next to theirs had been vacant for fifteen minutes; Carolyn had noticed Jesse and Suzann among those who had headed out the door instead of into the video games. When volleyball was through, it had been a smashing party, but Carolyn felt no compulsion to stick around.

Carolyn was the first one to Rose's house for the Relief Society presidency meeting Sunday morning. Elaine, the secretary, arrived a few minutes later. Suzann apologized as she walked in late.

"We were about to send the hound dogs after you," said Rose, as Suzann sat next to Elaine on the couch. "We need a prayer. Carolyn?"

"Sure." Carolyn offered the prayer.

"Do you want the minutes now?" Elaine asked afterwards.

"Just a minute." Rose looked at her watch. "Five . . . four . . . three . . . two . . . one . . ." She pointed to Elaine, who smiled and started to read.

"Corrections? Revisions? Additions?" asked Rose after Elaine had concluded.

"They sound good to me," said Suzann.

Rose looked at Carolyn, who remained silent. "Okay. Then we'll go on to new business." She glanced down at her notes. "Carolyn, have all the food assignments been made for the lake trip in two weeks? What did we decide to have?"

"We're having chili dogs with cheese, chips, watermelon, and s'mores. Everything has been assigned, and Janice Freestone is going to call and remind everyone a week from Thursday."

"That sounds good. I'm sorry I have to work that night." Actually, Rose would only have been sorry to miss a lake trip if she had weighed about fifty pounds less. She returned to her pad. "Suzann, are the new Relief Society lists ready to be handed out next Sunday?"

"Tina Johnson has been working on those. She said she'd like another week."

"That's what she said last week. Shall we give it to her?"

"As long as she spells my name right, I'm willing to wait another week," answered Suzann.

"Okay. By the skin of her teeth she keeps the job. Now, what about August homemaking night? What do you have lined up for that?"

"We have four classes: 'cooking for two,' given by Sandra Stewart, and 'elegant sewing,' with Anna LeSuer offering tips for sewing with satins, silks, and other materials for special occasions. Then Debbie Rogers is demonstrating fabric wedding albums. They can hold other pictures, too. What else was there? Oh. Peggy Savage makes wedding cakes and is giving a demonstration."

"Is somebody getting married?" asked Carolyn.

"We're a singles' ward. Eventually somebody might," answered Suzann. "If there's a mini-class you'd like to see offered, let me know."

"I think if your emphasis is on weddings," stated Carolyn, "maybe you should give a class on how to catch a husband —in less than a month."

Suzann stared at Carolyn. "Wait a minute. Just in case I detect a little hostility, you're the one who dumped Jesse

Mitchell three weeks ago. Don't try to make me feel guilty."
There. Suzann had said it out loud. She had been telling it to
herself quite often the past few weeks.

"Dumped? You don't understand at all."

"Hold on," interrupted Rose softly. "I can't find Jesse
Mitchell anywhere on the agenda."

Carolyn flushed and looked down, burning her gaze into
the notebook spread across her lap. *Suzann's right,* she
thought. *I can't blame her. It's my own fault.*

When Suzann stood up after the meeting, Carolyn bolted
over to her. "Suzann, I'm sorry. I was rude."

"I'm sorry, too. I didn't want you to be hurt."

"I know. And I don't blame you. I really want you to be
happy."

Suzann stared into Carolyn's eyes. They were so intense,
blazing with conviction and sincerity. And pain.

"I didn't expect to become involved with Jesse," said
Suzann. "I called him because someone was breaking into my
house. It was the night he asked you to marry him. He thought
I was you. Sometimes I wonder if he still wishes I were."

"No." Carolyn was shaking her head. "I blew it with Jesse.
But I hope there's someone like him around when I'm ready to
say yes."

"I've never met anyone who had more guys hovering
around than you."

"Like Jesse?"

Suzann hesitated. "I hope when you're ready to say yes
you can find someone like him, too."

# 12

When she had a chance to think about it, Rose was relieved that Carolyn and Suzann seemed to have reconciled the conflict that had threatened their friendship and her presidency. But it wasn't until the next day that she had the chance to think about it, after she had extended and buckled her seat belt and watched an oxygen mask demonstration by the stewardess. Rose leaned into the stiff take-off-positioned backrest, inhaled the stale plane oxygen, and opened her mind to the matters which had been kept at bay by her vacation countdown.

At the pizza party, Rose had wondered whether Carolyn was as surprised as she was to find Jesse and Suzann together. She had wondered, too, if repercussions would be felt in their presidency meeting. When Jesse Mitchell had become the undercurrent of homemaking-night plans, Rose sensed an antagonism not appropriate in a Relief Society council. And yet, even while expelling Jesse from the discussion, she had questioned whether she was doing the right thing. While changing the subject might salvage the atmosphere of the meeting, it would only thwart any resolution of the conflict. But after the closing prayer, Carolyn and Suzann had caught each other and talked, and when they headed out the front door together, it was as if nothing more serious had disrupted their friendship than buying an identical dress or planning a party for the same night. Had Carolyn surrendered Jesse to

Suzann with her blessings? Rose didn't know. Maybe it would be her turn to have Jesse Mitchell next. The only thing that was certain was that love caused problems. A man could scramble your relationships, short-circuit your nervous system, and tie your heart into knots. Ask Suzann. Ask Carolyn. But a woman could do the same thing. Ask Earnie.

Earnie was an anesthesiologist. He knocked people out. He also was the spitting image of Tom Selleck. He knocked women out. He had pulled Rose aside five minutes before her shift was over Saturday night and said, "You've got to have dinner with me."

"But I've already eaten," Rose protested.

"You'll have to eat again. I really need to talk to you."

So three minutes later, Rose was following Earnie to the hospital cafeteria. He froze at the entrance. "No. Not here. I want some real food."

They had left the hospital in his Celica and driven across town to Barclay's, where Earnie put his name on an estimated twenty-minute waiting list. In the lounge, Rose felt that they attracted more attention than the band. Earnie was so stunning, everybody must be trying to figure out what he was doing with her. She knew people tended to be overly sensitive in social situations, but she had actually seen a girl point at them. She felt better after they had been escorted to a table.

"Is it Natalie?" Rose asked when it was quiet enough for a conversation.

"Natalie." Earnie nodded. "She wants to get married, but . . ."

"Don't do it."

"I really think . . . what?"

"Don't marry her."

"Why not?"

"A girl like Natalie could date every night. It wouldn't be fair to take her out of circulation."

"You're purposely confusing me. You don't need to. I'm already confused. Do you know what the chances are for a marriage to succeed these days? They give better odds in Las Vegas. It scares me."

"Temple marriages improve the odds."

"When I'm ready to join the Mormon church, you'll be the first to know. Right now, I'm wrestling with another decision . . . marriage." Earnie sighed. "If only Natalie weren't so beautiful. Isn't she beautiful?"

"She is," answered Rose. "Is she what you want in a wife?"

"I like to be with her."

"That's important. You'll have to be with her sometimes if you marry her."

He smiled. Rose smiled, too. "Do you want the same things out of life? Like children? A home of your own? Vacations on the beach?"

"I don't know. I think we'd both like an automatic garage-door opener." He was kidding. "We really haven't talked about things like that."

"Maybe it's time."

After the waitress stopped at their table, Earnie and Rose followed her directions to the salad bar.

"Colleen!" exclaimed Earnie, as he recognized a face at the table they were going by. He stopped to talk a minute before he and Rose pressed on to the vegetables.

"That was Natalie's sister," explained Earnie, while they filled their plates. "It's a good thing I was just with you or I might be in real trouble."

Rose hadn't challenged his words at the time, but now, on the plane, they bothered her. Was she so unattractive that when it came to luring away somebody's man, she was like a hook without bait? She shut out the thought and reached for the magazine that someone had left in the pocket of the seat in front of her. It was a *Glamour* magazine—the June issue with all the bathing suits. Rose stuffed it back into the pocket without opening it. But she wasn't totally disheartened. Here came the peanut and beverage tray down the isle.

As the pilot announced their descent, Rose regretted the fact that she had accepted her brother Bill's offer to spend four days with his family in Austin, Texas. He and his wife, Marie, always made her feel welcome, and their three daughters were sweet, but they inevitably set Rose up with some eligible bachelor from their stake. And each time they were sure this would be the match that would change her life, when usually all it did was spoil a little bit of her vacation.

The first Texan Rose had found herself paired with was a man who wrote sports articles for the Austin paper. The only thing they had in common was that they were both physically unattractive. When she was reporting back to her brother, she told Bill he was okay, but it was hard to get to know someone who wore a permanent radio earphone.

"You're kidding. He wore an earphone and didn't take it out?" Bill had exclaimed.

"No. But once he turned it down."

"The next guy I'm really going to screen," declared Bill.

"No. Please, Bill, you don't need to be my matchmaker. Besides, I'm serious about a guy back home."

But Bill hadn't believed her, and on her next visit there was someone else. This man seemed a little more promising. He taught art at the local high school, and Rose had always been interested in drawing and painting.

He took Rose to watch the local dramatic group's production of *Hello Dolly*. He had designed the scenery and had created some brilliant backdrops. After the play, he invited Rose to come to his home and see more of his artwork. "If you don't think it will bore you," he added.

"No, it sounds great," Rose responded enthusiastically. "I like looking at pictures. That's why I go to the state fair—for the art exhibits."

"Really? I go for the freak shows."

Rose laughed. He was kidding. He had a sense of humor. This guy was going to be all right.

As soon as he had Rose planted on the couch, he brought out thirteen portfolios of paintings. After two hours, they had gone through five of them. Because they were all abstract, he spent a lot of time explaining themes, color schemes, direction, and emotional response. After portfolio number six, Rose stood up and said, "I'll wait for you in the car." She couldn't think of anything more tactful at the time and yet knew she had to get out of there before he opened portfolio number seven.

"Different," Rose had explained him to her brother.

"But Marie's niece took an art class from him and said he was a great teacher."

"Maybe he is. He gives one thorough explanation. But as a date, he doesn't rate that high," said Rose. "Bill, please, no more mystery men."

But there had been more. A few really weren't so bad. There was one man Rose still thought about now and then. His name was Fred and he was working on his Ph.D. in psychology. "That's why I'm kind of crazy," he explained when they met. And kind of cute, decided Rose. Even though Fred was small and thin, he had an incredible smile.

After he helped her into his car, Rose found herself straddling a plain brown box which took up most of the leg room. The flaps stuck open and she peered inside. There was a wig and a skin cap, a pair of Groucho Marx and Atom Ant glasses, a clown nose, some goggles, a beard, a surgeon's mask, and what looked like a Superman cape.

"You can't fool me about being a psychology student," said Rose. "I've discovered your disguises. You're a detective, aren't you?"

Fred laughed. "My disguises. I keep them handy to liven things up a little now and then. But that box must be in your way. Next stoplight you can help me move it to the back seat."

Rose nodded, but the music coming from the speakers was seizing her attention. "That's not Alvin and the Chipmunks, is it?"

"Do you remember them?" Fred stopped for a red light and started to hoist the box to the back seat. Rose gave him a hand.

"I listened to the Chipmunks as a boy," he continued, "so I bought the tape on impulse, as a link to my childhood. When you have children you can buy things like that all the time. But I didn't know if the tape would still be on sale by the time I had kids."

"You did the right thing. I doubt if you could have even adopted in time," said Rose. "I remember hearing Alvin and the Chipmunks at my cousin's house."

"Well, today you're going to hear real animals. I thought we'd go to the zoo. My hobby is photography and I want to take some pictures. Does that sound okay?"

102

"Fine. Just don't aim the camera my way."

"I can't promise. When I see a good shot, I press the trigger."

Rose just looked at Fred. Was he kidding? Did he think she could make a good shot?

At the zoo, Fred talked to the animals as if they were high-fashion models.

"Okay, lion, I don't want a real big smile, just something sexy. Good. Now a half turn . . . beautiful." Click.

To the chimpanzee; "I want you to tone it down for this picture. We're trying to create 'somber' here. Come on. Hold still. Wipe off the grin. Think of something sad, like a truck just totalled your new Mercedes . . . with your girlfriend in it. You might even yield the hint of a tear. Never mind, you can give me playful. We'll work on somber with the turtle." Click.

Fred received funny looks from some of the other visitors, but he made Rose giggle.

After the zoo, they picked up a late lunch at Jack-in-the-Box. Fred started to pay for his order by handing the girl in the drive-through window his Sears charge card.

"It has to get boring doing that all day," he explained to Rose as they were pulling into traffic. "I try to give them a little diversion."

They took their food to the lake and watched sailboat races. Fred rooted for a boat with a blue-striped sail. When it took second place, he pulled Rose over with him to congratulate the owner, a ploy which earned them a ride. Rose had never been in a sailboat, but as she sat under the bright flapping sail, with the wind tangling her hair and the sun sending its rays right through her skin until she could feel the warmth deep inside, she could imagine what it was like to be one of the beautiful people. And when Fred smiled at her and called, "This is great!" she knew.

It was the kind of day that explained how others could talk about "dates" in glowing terms. It was the kind of day that made wearing a watch useless, since time was of such little consequence. But inevitably, Fred's car returned them to the home of her brother.

"Thanks for spending the day with me," Fred told her. "I didn't expect to have such a good time. That sounded wonderful, didn't it? But you know what I mean; blind dates are like playing roulette . . . and you're probably thinking, 'Yeah, and my marble landed on a real nut.' "

Rose couldn't believe someone was talking to her this way. It was practically like flirting. "After you warned me you were a little crazy, I would have been disappointed if you hadn't displayed nut-like tendencies."

"Nut-like tendencies, huh? I noticed some in you, too. Like when I opened the door to help you out at the zoo, you had my World War I flying ace goggles on."

Rose smiled.

"I liked being with you, Rose."

She could practically feel the smile reaching to her ears. It was an involuntary nervous system smile, to think that somebody appreciated the qualities in her that didn't show up in the mirror. But as they said good-bye, Fred didn't ask to see her again or how to get in touch with her. Afterwards, Rose decided she had just been another experiment.

The plane stopped. As Rose dragged her purse from under the seat where she had tucked it, she wondered who it would be this trip.

Bill was waiting alone for Rose. His girls enjoyed coming to the airport, but he had stopped on his way from work.

"Rose!" He pulled her into a bear hug. "You made it."

"So far. But the dangerous part of the trip hasn't started yet. Do you still drive like a 16-year-old in that Camaro of yours?"

"No. I bought a 'Vette. Wait 'til you see how I weave through traffic."

"I won't ask how business is, then, if you just bought a new 'Vette."

"It was two years old. That means business is real good, but not great."

On the drive home, Bill came three inches from running into a van that turned in front of him. When Rose opened her eyes, she said, "I should have taken a taxi." But five minutes later, Bill pulled safely into his drive.

The girls, who had been watching for them from the front window, shot out the door to greet their favorite aunt. They didn't mention the presents, but they knew they were planted in Rose's suitcase.

Marie, Bill's wife, was waiting, too, just inside the house. "We're so glad you could come."

Rose unpacked in the guest room. She called the girls in as she was hanging up her clothes and handed them small square packages. Books, they guessed, and they were right in a way. Inside were books with blank pages—journals. The girls were delighted, calling out "Thank you" before rushing off to search for pens.

When Rose emerged from the guest room, Bill told her, "We thought you'd just want to take it easy tonight, after traveling." But Rose was suspicious. He'd suggested spending the evening at home before, and a single male friend had just happened to drop by. She expected to hear the doorbell ring while Bill was grilling hamburgers in the backyard.

Later in the evening Marie started making nachos and virgin piña coladas. Rose read it as a sign that company was coming. When the girls asked her to play Killer Uno, a card game, she hesitated, because she didn't know how soon "he" would be here. But they coaxed until she cried, "Deal me in."

Two hours later, after the last Killer Uno hand, after the nachos and piña coladas had been consumed, there had been no visitor. *He's giving me a break,* decided Rose. *Bill has saved Cupid for tomorrow night.*

Rose spent the next day with Marie and the girls. She drew some posters for Marie's Relief Society lesson and drove with them to take Marie's mother some peaches which had already been bottled. In the afternoon, Rose read while Marie and the girls went swimming.

When Bill came home from work, he was escorting a baby-sitter to watch the girls while the adults went out for dinner. Rose didn't wonder what restaurant they would eat at or what kind of food would be served. Rose wondered who Bill had lined up to fill in the foursome. She had been introduced twice to potentials while going out to dinner. But this time the fourth water glass remained unturned.

The final night Rose was to be in Texas, Bill's ward was having an adult activity—a dinner and square dance. He and Marie had been on the planning committee, so Bill felt obligated to go, but he gave Rose the option. Since Rose knew this must be the night Bill had arranged for her to meet someone, she accepted so she wouldn't spoil his plans.

Throughout the western dinner—the chili and cornbread and coleslaw—Rose scanned the room for the man who had been lined up to be her partner. She was debating over several when empty plates started being gathered from the tables.

"Do you want to participate in the square dancing, Rose?" Bill asked. "We weren't sure if you'd be interested so we didn't line you up with a partner, but if you'd like to dance we'll find somebody for you."

"Sure. I'll dance," answered Rose. *Play along with it.*

After several minutes, Bill was back. "There doesn't seem to be an odd man out tonight," he explained.

Rose had been sure this was going to be the setup. "What?"

"Bill, you start out dancing with Rose," said Marie, "I need to help in the kitchen for a while."

So there had been no blind date waiting for her in Texas. By the time she boarded the flight that would take her back home, Rose had been introduced to not one prospective husband. She should have felt relieved. And yet, as Rose buckled her seatbelt and listened once more to the oxygen mask demonstration, she felt depressed. *Bill's given up on me. I'm a zero threat factor to Earnie's girlfriend, and Bill, too, has finally realized I'm hopeless.*

The stewardess was coming down the aisle, making sure all the seats were in take-off position.

"Rose!"

Rose startled at hearing her name. She looked closely at the uniformed young woman who had just addressed her. "Lindsey?"

"Yes. It's me. If I get a second I'll come back and say 'hi,' " she answered, then turning to the man behind Rose, "Please put your seat all the way up, sir."

It was fifteen minutes later when Lindsey came and sat in the empty seat by Rose. "I still remember when you changed your lines in *Cinderella*."

"Why does everyone always remember that? That performance has practically made me famous."

"You shocked all of us. But that was a long time ago. What are you up to now? How many children do you have?"

"Maybe you'd better ask how many husbands I have first."

Lindsey laughed. "How stupid of me. But you always seemed like the type to settle down with a family. I mean, you just seemed motherly. I was the flighty one, and would you believe it? I'm married with two boys."

"Times have changed for a stewardess. They used to be single."

"I guess times change for everyone. What do you do?"

"I'm a nurse. I've been working in a hospital emergency room."

"Really? How exciting. I wish I could hear about it, but I have to get back."

"It was good to see you," said Rose. "I like your hair short like that. I almost didn't recognize you."

"You like it? My husband's still hurt because I didn't keep it long. Men!" She shook her head as she stood up and walked away.

Men. They caused problems. Rose wouldn't mind having some of those problems. But the real problem was that first one had to say, "I love you."

# 13

Tyler, Janice, and Josh were back. Alice's father-in-law was sent to the hospital by a heart attack three days before the Forty-ninth Ward lake trip, and while Alice, her husband, and the baby spent a few days at his side in Salt Lake City, their older children returned to the home of Carolyn and her parents. It was easier adjusting to the children a second time. The system of dos and don'ts, cans and can'ts was already laid out; it only had to be reinforced. Not that new situations didn't periodically arise which had to be defined and decided upon— like the lake trip. It fell exactly on Tyler's fifth birthday. And what he wanted, more than seeing a movie or having a cake, was going to the lake with Carolyn.

"Tyler, I'm not even sure I'm going," said Carolyn. She didn't look forward to seeing how the courtship of Jesse and Suzann was progressing. Still Jesse. *He still holds my heart,* thought Carolyn, *like a kid who put something in his pocket and then forgot about it. But he still has it with him.*

"Albert next door has a boat, and I went with them once to the lake. And it went so fast. And it was so much fun. I think it was the most fun I've ever had in my whole life." Tyler's eyes were shining and his face was tense with anticipation.

There would be plenty of boats, and probably even other children there. Usually some of the single parents brought their kids to ward activities.

Tyler could sense that Carolyn was wavering. "I can

borrow Albert's life vest. Albert's a little bigger than me, but it fits me perfect. It probably even fits me better than Albert."

Carolyn laughed. He was trying so hard. And it would be his birthday.

At four o'clock Carolyn left with Tyler, who was wearing Albert's life vest. Windows down, radio humming, seat belts on—Carolyn glanced over at Tyler, who was adjusting the straps of Albert's vest. She was glad she had company for the drive. And Tyler would keep her preoccupied. So preoccupied she wouldn't even notice Jesse and Suzann.

After Carolyn had pulled into the lake parking area, Tyler carried their towels and she brought a sack of hot dogs down to the dock. A boat from their group was preparing to launch.

"Hi, Carolyn!" called a friend, lounging comfortably in a big beige ski boat.

Carolyn and Tyler climbed up to join her.

"Who wants to ski?" asked Greg Baily at the wheel of the boat, after they had passed the no-wake buoys.

Carolyn let the silence stretch almost into a minute before she spoke up. "I will. I can't pass up a dry life jacket." She kicked the thongs from her feet, stripped off her cutoffs and oxford shirt, and pulled the life jacket over her bathing suit.

"One ski or two?" asked Greg, pointing to a pocket in the side where the skis were kept.

"One. But let me adjust it first." Carolyn fit the foothold to her size. Before she dived into the water, she cautioned Tyler, "Just sit right there and watch."

The water temperature was tepid, perfect for a summer evening. Carolyn intercepted the ski which had been launched in her direction and then swam to the ski rope that had come flying through the air. She was ready when the boat shifted from neutral to high gear. The rope tightened, pulling the strength from her arms, straining her muscles—*hold on*—drawing her out of the water. She was up. Skiing. Gliding through the deep green glass. She loved the warm air that poured over her body. She loved the mountains that nestled the lake and the voluptuous clouds that reflected the water and later would glow with the colors of the sunset.

Carolyn jumped the wake and started darting from one

side of the boat to the other. The feel of the grips and the pressure and the water were familiar, even though Carolyn hadn't been skiing for a long time. Too long. When the boat pulled into a cove and neared the beach where the ward was gathering, Carolyn tossed up the rope and coasted into shore.

There were several boats and a good-sized crowd. Some people were loading into the boats for a chance to ride or ski; others were waiting on the beach where quilts had been spread out. Before Carolyn joined those on the beach, she handed her ski back to Greg, who had docked, and collected her clothes, towels, hot dogs, and nephew.

"Tyler, I need to go take a food inventory." They were on the shore and Carolyn was stepping into her clothes. "I don't want you to go near the water. Promise?"

"But I have the life vest on. I won't drown."

"I know, but boats will be coming in and out. Just stay back."

Bags of food were scattered around the camp, and Carolyn started to gather them together on one quilt near where they would be barbecuing. While she was organizing, she could hear the whine of an arriving boat. A few minutes later, Suzann was greeting her and setting a bag next to the others.

"Hi," said Suzann. "Looks like there's going to be enough food."

"There better be. The nearest grocery store is fifteen miles away."

"Shall we get out some chips and let people start munching?" asked Suzann. "I brought some stuff to mix up a guacamole dip. Maybe I'll do that now."

"Carolyn! Come on!" Tyler was squeaking from near the water. When Carolyn pinpointed the voice, she could only attach it to a torso. From the waist down, Tyler was submerged in the lake, standing next to the boat which had pulled in a minute ago.

Carolyn dashed to him. "Tyler!"

"Let's climb in," he cried. "They're about to take off."

Steve Marshall was dangling a hand over the bow. "Need some help?"

Tyler grabbed the hand and walked up the side of the boat.

"Push us off a little, Carolyn, before I help you in," said Steve.

Carolyn lunged towards them, springing her feet from the shore and propelling the boat backwards. As the motor started spitting into gear, she let Steve's iron grip lift her out of the water and into the boat.

"Thanks." She turned to Tyler with a scowl. "Tyler, you told me you wouldn't go by the water. I expect . . ."

"I'm sorry, Carolyn. I just wanted to see Jesse."

Carolyn scanned the boat. Its occupants included Steve, Chip Smith in the driver's seat, Ann Barlow, and, in the back, untangling a snarl of ski rope, Jesse.

"Your turn, Ann," Steve told Ann, pointing to the skis.

"Wait. I don't know. I've never skied before. Jesse, there's no hurry with the rope."

"Too late." Jesse was coiling the rope loosely around one arm. "The rope's ready. No more stalling."

Jesse's voice. Carolyn looked around. Why didn't anyone else seem to be jolted by it? His voice arrested her as if his words were pieces of a brilliant speech. This was ridiculous.

"You can do it, Ann," coaxed Chip. "We'll be barking out instruction. It'll be easy."

"I don't know."

"Steve, throw her in." Chip might have been kidding, but Steve looked as if the idea appealed to him.

"Wait. I'll do it. Give me the skis. Let me see if they fit."

When Ann had dived into the water, Carolyn reached for the bright orange flag by her feet.

"Can I hold it?" asked Tyler.

"Okay. Hold it real high. The flag tells the other boats we have a skier in the water. Maybe you should take it to the back of the boat. You can watch the skier better from there."

"I can watch her from up here. I like to ride in the front better. It's windier. I'll go back later and say 'hi' to Jesse."

Even though Ann had been bombarded by suggestions, she didn't make it out of the water her first try. She didn't make it out her second try. But the third try, she was up for five seconds before she toppled over.

"This time I'm going to do it," Ann told them when they circled around her, bringing the ski rope.

As the boat mustered speed and dragged her through the water, Ann held on. She was up. She was standing. She was skiing. Cheers erupted from the boat. Carolyn jumped to her feet and clapped over her head.

"Tyler, you can put down the flag," Carolyn turned from Ann to Tyler. He was leaning over the bow, straining. Reaching. He slipped over the front of the boat, into the water.

"Tyler fell in!" cried Carolyn.

They all were watching Ann. Over the roar of the engine, no one could hear her. And Tyler was under the boat.

Carolyn jumped next to Chip and cut the motor. Tyler had already passed underneath and could be seen from the rear. Bobbing in the lake behind the boat, his body was slowly being enveloped in a rust-colored cloud. He had been sliced by the propeller.

Jesse dived from the stern and carefully pulled Tyler back to the boat. When he lifted him to Carolyn, the way Tyler's head flopped back set off a siren in her mind. "Tyler!"

He was unconscious. Was he breathing? Jesse had climbed aboard and was checking for vital signs. "He's breathing. He has a weak pulse. He was knocked out by the boat. We need to get him to the hospital."

Carolyn had found the source of his bleeding, a cut through the life jacket by his right shoulder, and she ripped off her shirt to press against the wound and slow the loss of blood.

Steve was helping Ann and the skis back into the boat. As soon as she had both legs inside, Chip launched full speed toward the dock. Carolyn cradled Tyler in her arms. "You're going to be okay, Tyler. Please. Be okay."

When they landed, Jesse jumped down and ran to his car. He was back in a minute, and Carolyn lowered Tyler into his arms.

"Would you tell Suzann where I am?" Jesse asked Ann before he carried Tyler to Carolyn, who was already in his front seat.

They were on the highway. The only music came from the engine. Jesse was driving fast. Faster than Carolyn could have comfortably driven, but he appeared to be in control. As always. She watched his dark eyes set on the road and traced his profile with an imaginary finger. She could almost forget something was wrong, being so close to Jesse. But Tyler's body was limp and cool in her arms.

Carolyn held Tyler closer. She wished she had a towel to wrap around him. Mingled with the smell of blood and lake water was Tyler's scent, and recognizing it released a tear down her cheek.

"Is he still losing blood?" asked Jesse.

"Not as much as before." Carolyn had just checked the soggy shirt a few seconds earlier. The swaying of the car along the winding road and the smell of blood were making her nauseous.

"Good. We'll be there soon."

Tyler opened his eyes, "Jesse?"

"Tyler. How do you feel?"

"Jesse, are you playing the dwarfs? I can hear the dwarfs." Tyler's voice was weak.

"No. We're riding in the car."

"You and me and Carolyn? Are we going somewhere fun like you said we would? Are we going to ride horses?"

Jesse drew in a breath. "No. This isn't the time I told you about."

"Carolyn, my arm hurts."

"I know. We're going right now to fix it."

"It hurts, it hurts," he was whispering. His eyes were closing.

Tyler was out for the rest of the drive. He was out when Jesse carried him into the emergency room.

"I need to talk with someone about insurance," said a nurse at the desk.

"They need you," Jesse told Carolyn. "I'll go with Tyler."

An attendant pointed Jesse to a bed walled by curtains on three sides. As soon as Jesse laid Tyler down, Rose Adams swung around the corner and into the cubicle. Only for a moment did her eyes flash with alarm; then she worked quickly, calmly.

The doctor was in and out, but it was mostly Rose who administered to Tyler. Jesse watched her nimble fingers thread the I.V. and in one swift jab attach it to Tyler's wrist. When she started to swab his cut, Tyler moaned and became alert. Rose let him squeeze her hand while she whispered softly that in a minute it would be all over. The smell of the disinfectant and Tyler's first glimpse of the wound made him nauseous. Rose was there with a towel. Watching Rose was like watching anyone who performed a skill proficiently. In her movements he saw the grace of a dancer, the expediency of a poet, the endurance of a runner.

Carolyn joined Jesse just before the doctor confronted them.

"I need to take some X rays," said the doctor. "I want to check his head where he was bumped, and also the shoulder. He'll need stitches, too. If you want to follow us, I'll show you where you can wait."

Tyler was awake and frightened; Carolyn talked to him as he was wheeled down the hall. The doctor pointed out a small waiting room. It was empty except for a man reading in the corner. Carolyn patted Tyler good-bye and headed for the waiting room's drinking fountain. Jesse followed her.

Carolyn realized her bathing suit was covered only by her cutoffs. "Look how I'm dressed," she said after a short drink.

"Do you want my shirt?"

"I don't know. You need it, too," Carolyn answered. "Tyler looked okay, didn't he? Do you think he'll be all right?"

"Oh, yeah. He'll be fine."

"I never realized how precious he is, until I was holding him in my arms. Until I was afraid of losing him. I thought how much potential there is in one little child. How eager they are to learn and understand and grow up, and what a privilege it is to help them. I never realized how much I loved him until tonight. I never realized how much I loved you." Carolyn closed her eyes. "I didn't mean to say that. I know you've been seeing Suzann."

She felt the warmth of Jesse's arms wrapping around her, drawing her closer and closer. She was going to be crushed. But it was okay. They were Jesse's arms. He held her for a long time. Neither made an attempt to relax the embrace.

Jesse and Carolyn were startled apart by a voice from the corner: "It's hard, isn't it?" The man had set down his book and was looking at them. He continued, "I saw them wheel your little boy by. My wife's being operated on, too. She's been in for almost two hours. I'm going crazy out here waiting."

"I'll bet she's with a really good doctor in there," said Carolyn.

"He's the best." The man nodded. He smoothed back what was left of his hair. "But you never know . . . and it was only yesterday we were just like you. Just starting out, with all the years in the world ahead of us."

"The doctors these days—they can practically work miracles," said Jesse. He and Carolyn sat in chairs next to the man.

"I'm hoping."

While the afflictions of their loved ones were being attended, they talked about the humidity, about who would take the baseball pennant this year, and about the blockbuster historical novel that was currently airing as a TV mini-series.

"The trouble with TV movies that go on for five nights," said Jesse, "is that I'm only home maybe for two of those nights. And who wants to watch two segments of a five-part series?"

"Do you work nights? What kind of business are you in? asked the man.

"I've been putting together some computer program packages for accounting firms. How about you?"

"I'm an assistant editor at the *Herald.*"

"Is that right? Carolyn is working towards her degree in communications," said Jesse.

"You want to be a journalist?" he asked Carolyn.

"I want to write. It doesn't have to be in a newsroom. It could be something I did at home, you know, and raise a family, too."

Carolyn's father stuck his head in the door.

"Dad!"

"Carolyn." He greeted Jesse and walked over to give his daughter a hug. "How's Tyler?"

"He's getting some stitches now," Carolyn answered. "I think he'll be okay."

"Your mom wanted to come, too, but Josh is already in bed. Did you get the insurance straightened out?"

"Mom said to just write a check for the hospital bill and we could be reimbursed by the insurance company when we found out who it was."

Shortly after Carolyn's father had joined them, the doctor returned. "The boy is doing well," he said. "We stitched his shoulder. I was afraid we were going to find a slashed tendon in there, but it was all right. He's just going to be a little sore. He's had a slight concussion and we'd like to keep him here the rest of the night."

"Can we see him?" asked Carolyn.

"We put him out for the stitches and he's still unconscious."

After speaking with the doctor, Carolyn's father said he would stay with Tyler and suggested she take his car home. Carolyn left her father and walked with Jesse down the hospital corridor.

"I think Tyler dropped the ski flag in the lake," she said. "He fell in trying to retrieve it."

"I saw the flag in the water. That must have been it."

"I was in charge of the dinner at the lake tonight. I hope it went on just the same without me."

"Some things don't go on just the same without you, Carolyn, but I suspect dinners aren't one of them. I doubt if anyone will starve."

*Some things don't go on the same without me?*

Carolyn stopped just before they were leaving the hospital, as they passed the entrance to the emergency room. "Uh-oh, I'm about to do something really stupid."

"I can't wait. What?"

"Try to start my dad's car without the keys. Just a minute. I'll run back and get them."

After Carolyn had turned to go, the emergency door opened and Rose started to walk out.

"Rose!" Jesse grabbed her by the shoulders. "Have I ever told you you're beautiful? I love you!" He was smiling at her. The smile was reflected in all of his features. After he had admired her, he pulled her into his arms and squeezed her. When Jesse turned Rose loose, she stumbled back against the wall. She gave him a weak smile and mumbled that she was on her way to get something, then disappeared through another door.

116

Carolyn was back.

"Rose was wonderful with Tyler. I just saw her."

"When?" asked Carolyn.

"A second ago, while you went for the keys."

"No. When was she wonderful with Tyler?"

"She worked on him in the emergency room."

"Really?"

"I wouldn't lie about something like that."

Jesse walked Carolyn to her father's car.

"Thank you, Jesse. You were there again when I needed you."

"You know the Scout motto."

"Always be prepared?"

"The other one. Be ready to come to Carolyn's aid."

Carolyn smiled. They were staring at each other. Jesse lifted his hand as if he were going to stroke her hair the way he used to, and pull her head to his shoulder. But he stopped. He glanced at the clock on her father's dashboard. It read 7:05. "I need to get back to the lake." He took a step backwards, but his eyes were reluctant to leave her face.

"See you, Jesse."

"See you, Carolyn."

She watched him walk away.

# 14

Rose had watched Jesse walk away, too, through a small rectangle of glass as she stood in a room full of medical supplies. Still astonished, she turned her mind back to the scene which had just transpired. Jesse had said she was beautiful. Not becoming, not cute, not attractive—beautiful. And his eyes weren't lying, either. She couldn't exactly see her reflection in his pupils, but if she could have, she knew that the woman captured in those round, black frames in his penetrating eyes would have been beautiful. Then he had said those words. The words no man whose last name didn't match her own had ever spoken to her: "I love you." Even repeated by her own mind, they gave her a rush. And the hug. His strong, warm arms, pressing her to him, sealing the impact of his message. Now she had experienced it. A brief version of the American love scene. And the fruit she had stopped jumping for was sweet.

Rose replaced a bottle of Demerol and some extra bandages on the supply shelves, then spent her break looking for Natalie. She spotted the particular white uniform she was looking for on the second-floor nurse's station.

"Natalie, who was that orthodontist you said your sister was going to—the one she likes so much?"

"Oh, hi, Rose," answered Natalie. "I think his last name was Brackin. You aren't thinking about having your teeth fixed, are you?"

"Isn't it about time?"

"I don't know. Once you get used to the way someone looks, it really doesn't matter."

*This from a raving beauty,* thought Rose. "Natalie," she answered, "I ran on that ticket for a long time, convincing myself that looks aren't the ultimate. And I still believe they aren't. But somewhere in the campaign I decided that neglecting my appearance was part of the program. I don't believe that anymore."

"What changed your mind?"

Rose thought a minute. "A reflection I almost saw in a pair of eyes." Rose didn't seem to notice the puzzled look that Natalie gave her. "And one day, I'm going to see that reflection in the mirror . . . Take a good look at this uniform, Natalie, because in a few weeks, it's going to be too big."

Walking back down the hall, Rose remembered again her transaction with Jesse. Again she felt the confused elation of eyes bursting with approval drilling into her own. Again she was warmed by an embrace she had been released from almost fifteen minutes ago. Again she heard the words. Rose smiled. *So I got to hear the words after all. One day, I just might hear them again.*

# 15

It was perfect. That's what Suzann had determined after she sampled a small glob of guacamole from her fingertip. *Jesse will like it.* The last time she had made a guacamole dip, Jesse couldn't leave it alone; that's why she had decided to make some for the lake. She set the bowl down next to a bag of potato chips and looked around. No Jesse. He must have gone back out with the boat. She made a second scan. There had to be someone else here she could slide into a conversation with until Jesse returned. But all the faces looked unfamiliar and 18. Suzann felt alone. Awkward. She wished Rose *wasn't* working and was here to talk to. Even more, she wished Jesse would hurry and come back; there was never enough time to be with him.

Suzann folded to a sit at the edge of a quilt and drew in the sand with a twig. She was preoccupied with her design until she heard the whine of an approaching boat and jerked her head up in anticipation. When she realized it wasn't Jesse's boat, she returned to her artwork in the sand. It was several minutes before she was interrupted again, this time by Elaine, the Relief Society secretary.

"Hi, Suzann. The water's perfect. Have you been skiing yet?"

"Not yet."

"I had to get my skiing in early," continued Elaine. "I'm playing tennis later tonight. Boy, the water's nice. Choppy in some places, but you can find smooth stretches, too. The

120

boat's just getting ready to take off again. Why don't you join them?"

"I'm waiting for Jesse. He went out with another boat and should be back any time."

"Jesse, huh? Are you two getting serious?"

"Yes. We're about ready to announce that we're seeing each other."

Elaine smiled, "Why doesn't anyone like to give a straight answer to that question?"

"Because it would dampen speculation." Suzann didn't add that right now her interpretation of Jesse's feelings was mostly speculation, too. He had made no bold confession of love or commitment, and yet there was something, like the way he watched her when she pretended not to notice, that made her wonder if she wasn't working her way into his heart.

Elaine was trying some guacamole on a chip. "This is delicious."

"Thanks," answered Suzann, but she was watching the boat that had just turned into the cove.

"Did you make the dip?"

"Yes." Suzann was trying to pick out Jesse. It was the boat that had brought them into the cove, so he had to be on it. She blinked and resumed her search.

"Did you put some lemon juice in to preserve the color?" asked Elaine.

Why didn't she see Jesse on the boat? "Ummm, a little."

"Yeah, that's what I do, too," replied Elaine.

The boat jammed into the sand without Jesse. Steve was securing it by tying the rope around a dead tree on shore.

"Carolyn's nephew fell into the water," Steve was telling a gathering group. "We didn't even know he'd gone in. His shoulder was slashed by the propeller."

"Is he okay?" someone asked.

"I don't know. They took him to the hospital. He was unconscious. I hope he's okay. He was breathing and all that." The others had unloaded by now and Steve turned to Ann, adding more quietly, "You need to tell Suzann."

Suzann stiffened at the sound of her name. Tell Suzann what? Did Jesse jump in to save the boy? Was he slashed by the propeller too?

Ann caught Suzann's face in the crowd and stumbled over to her. "Suzann, Jesse went with Carolyn to take her nephew to the hospital."

"Oh. Thanks," Suzann replied casually, as if something inside her hadn't just collapsed. *He's gone. But just to the hospital. No; not just to the hospital. He's really gone.* Suzann tried to shake the premonition, to convince herself she was being skeptical, but the feeling of loss clung to her. She wanted to escape—escape from her fears or at least from all these people. She wanted to wait it out alone. How long could she keep the mounting anxiety hidden beneath the disguise of a young woman having a splendid time at the lake?

"When're we gonna eat?" asked Chip.

Someone was thinking about food at a time like this. Suzann couldn't have felt more apathetic to the promptings from her stomach. It was a good thing she wasn't in charge. Who was? Carolyn. Carolyn, whose nephew was on his way to the hospital.

"We'll eat a lot sooner if we start the charcoal," replied Suzann. She pointed. "All the stuff is right over there. How about it, Chip?"

It was under Suzann's direction that dinner proceeded smoothly. She would much rather be preoccupied arranging a chili-dog assembly line than thinking about Jesse and Carolyn together tonight . . . Carolyn would be distraught and helpless, and Jesse would be comforting her. *Stop! Where are the chopped onions?*

The Forty-ninth Warders had progressed to dessert, sandwiching chocolate pieces and gooey roasted marshmellows between graham crackers, when Suzann's ears picked up Elaine asking for a ride back to the dock, saying she had to leave early.

"Can I get a ride with you?" Suzann approached Elaine. "I need to get back, too."

"Sure."

Elaine had a little Triumph convertible. Suzann was glad the rush of air in the car made it difficult to talk, but still Elaine attempted conversation.

"I'm meeting Stan at eight," Elaine said. "I think I can get there in time."

"You're playing tennis, right?" Suzann forced herself to be sociable.

"Yeah. We're in a doubles tournament next week. Usually I just enter as a single, but Stan talked me into it and it should be fun. I still think, though, your strength has to be in your singles game. You have to be comfortable on the court by yourself before you can be an effective partner. Do you know what I mean?"

Suzann was barely listening. "What?"

"I said most important is how you are as a single. That always comes first. You have to be able to feel like you can carry it alone before you team up with someone."

"Who, me?" Was Elaine still talking about tennis?

"Yes. Anyone. Do you play tennis?"

"No."

Suzann was laden with lake gear when she stepped out of Elaine's parked car in front of her house. She had her towel and purse and tennis shoes and mini-ice chest and bag of left-overs—all the things Jesse had helped her with when they were leaving for the lake. Elaine offered assistance, but Suzann declined it because she thought she could make it. Now, not quite at the door, she wasn't sure. After she had tottered up the steps and onto the porch, she rang the doorbell with her elbow. She could hear the radio blasting inside. *Somebody open the door. Trisha. Kevin. Come on. Open the door.*

Not only were Suzann's arms threatening to drop everything, but here came Mr. Yates from down the street—Mr. Yates, the master of idle conversation. With her hair blown into a snarly mess of witch hair and wearing her bathing suit, Suzann wasn't eager for a confrontation, but even more disturbing was the idea of being snared into an endless conversation.

Suzann hit the doorbell again. *Come on. Open the door.* As Mr. Yates approached, her urgency increased, and as her urgency increased, she had the distinct feeling she had been here before. It reminded her of something significant, but she couldn't narrow it down to what.

"Suzann!" Mr. Yates was closing in on her. She smiled in acknowledgement. As she attempted to lean against the doorbell one more time, she hit the door instead; it swung open, dropping her into the living room. From her sitting position, she shoved the door closed.

The contents of her arms had scattered on the carpet, but her first move was to turn off the stereo. It was the silence, not her desperate ringing, that pulled her children and their babysitter, Jackie, from upstairs.

"Hi, Mom," said Trisha. "Jackie was teaching us how to dance."

"I thought you were being punished with the Chinese eardrum torture."

"The music has to be real loud," Trisha explained, indulging her mother's ignorance. "You can't just hear it. You have to *feel* it, too. Right, Jackie?"

"For totally effective dancing," confirmed the expert.

"I don't know," Suzann resisted. "When you have the music that loud, you can't even hear yourself scream. Much less the doorbell."

Suzann started gathering her lake gear. When she came to her purse, she fished out some bills and handed them to Jackie. "Do you need a ride home?"

"No. I have my bike."

"Okay. Thanks."

After Jackie had gone, the children watched Suzann put things away.

"You guys forgot to remind Jackie to keep the door locked while I was gone," Suzann said.

"We did?" asked Trisha.

"Mmmm hmmm." Suzann hadn't explained about the burglar who entered their house, but she had started stressing precautions.

Suddenly, Trisha, whose physical demonstrations of affection had been on the decline, threw her arms around Suzann, knocking her mother off balance. Kevin, prompted as much by Trisha's action as a deep stirring within, followed his sister and embraced their mom.

124

Suzann knelt down and gathered them into her arms. "Thanks. What did I do to earn such big hugs?"

"You came home," answered Trisha. "We thought you'd be gone until we were asleep like when you usually go out with Jesse. I'm glad you decided to be with us."

"I've been gone a lot, haven't I?" Suzann asked.

"A real lot," said Kevin. "We like Jesse and everything, but you're with him more than you are us."

Suzann almost replied, "I think that will be changing," but how did she know? He was just helping Carolyn out. Someone had to assist in taking her nephew to the hospital; it just happened to be Jesse.

No. Somehow she knew.

"If you let me take a quick shower, when I'm through we can all do something together. Whatever you decide."

"Anything in the whole world?" asked Trisha.

"Anything in the living room," qualified Suzann, but even with the restriction her children were willing to bargain.

Suzann stood with the warm pelting droplets of the shower aimed at her body. What she really longed to do was wash her mind. She didn't want to go through this again. Not the loss, not the rejection, not the pain. It had been almost unbearable when Peter left, and although she and Jesse had never even talked about marriage, she couldn't help believing he was the one. He was everything she wanted. Jesse made every prospective husband list she had ever conceived look incomplete. He was the one who was going to save her from the lonely, floundering state of being single. He had already tossed out the rope that offered romance and excitement. But now, with a feeling that transcended suspicion, she knew the life preserver Jesse held wasn't going to be for her.

When Suzann had dressed, combed through her wet hair, and returned downstairs, Trisha was standing on a chair by the game closet. "Are we old enough to play Monopoly, Mom? I'd really like to play Monopoly."

"I don't know. Why don't we go with a simpler game like Candyland or Parcheesi?"

"No. Let's play Monopoly. You said anything in the living room. You can help Kevin."

"Okay. We'll try it."

Actually, Kevin didn't need a lot of help because he fell asleep on the couch while Suzann was still explaining to Trisha about buying matching properties and loading them with houses and hotels. Trisha was resolved to master the game, and when the shoe she chose as a marker stepped out from "Go," it was with a brisk gait.

Trisha's shoe and Suzann's hat worked their way around the board, snatching up properties. When Suzann landed on a bright pink question mark, Trisha teased, "You gonna buy it?"

Suzann smiled. "When you land on that you pick up one of these orange cards. They bring you good news, like you've won a beauty contest so you get to collect money from the bank."

Suzann picked up an orange card, wincing as she read.

"What's the good news?" asked Trisha.

"It isn't always good news. This says, 'Go directly to jail. Do not pass go. Do not collect 200 dollars.' "

Trisha was delighted. Not with her mother's misfortune, but because she recognized the expression. "That's what you say when you send us to our rooms. 'Do not pass go. Do not collect 200 dollars'!"

"No wonder it sounds familiar."

As Suzann moved her hat behind bars, she came to her own recognition. Maybe her subconscious had been working on it and only now was able to supply her with the answer. It was the dream. Standing outside, waiting to come in, had reminded her of that reoccurring nightmare in which someone was chasing her. Outside her childhood home, burdened with a child, she would cry desperately for someone to open the door. Then tonight she had wanted someone to open the door, too. No one had come. No one had come, but she had opened the door herself.

*I let myself in.* Suzann turned it over in her mind. *I thought I had to have someone, but I didn't. Do I have to have someone? I've been waiting for Peter to come back, suspending my life in anticipation of his return. The moment I realized he wasn't going to, I geared up for the dating game to find someone to take his place—someone to make me want to be*

*me again, someone to supply the missing pieces so I could
feel complete.*

"Mom . . ."

Suzann rolled a three and an eight. She couldn't move.
*Then Jesse entered, the rainbow after the storm. He was
going to do it for me. He was going to bring all the colors back
into my life. But now that prospect looks bleak, too. Do I
plunge into the search for someone else? Do I have to have
someone? Can't I just be Suzann, alone, with Trisha and
Kevin? What was that Elaine said? Something about a
singles game. You need to learn how to play singles first. You
have to strengthen your singles game before you can make
an effective partner. My strategy had been just the opposite.
I've tried to avoid the singles game. But it's me alone, first. I
have to be able to make my life meaningful and fulfilling just
by myself. Even if it's only me and Trisha and Kevin, my life
is going to be whole. My life is going to be good.*

"You rolled doubles, Mom. You're free."

Suzann looked down at the dice she had just thrown. She
actually felt free.

Just as Trisha bought her third house for Pennsylvania
Avenue, the doorbell rang. Suzann jumped up to answer it.

"Jesse." She hadn't expected Jesse. She had almost convinced herself she would never see him again. "Come in. Is
Carolyn's nephew okay?"

"Yes. He had a concussion and some stitches in his shoulder, but he'll be okay." Jesse smiled at Trisha. "Who is that
with all the houses over there?"

"It's me. We're playing Monopoly. Do you want to play?
We can start over."

"Monopoly isn't the kind of game you start over. If you
keep starting over in Monopoly, it could go on for weeks,"
answered Jesse. "But maybe you'd take me on as your finan-
cial advisor."

Jesse played with Trisha against Suzann until Trisha
joined Kevin in slumber on the couch. Now it was just the two
adults, sole survivors in the real estate market. Jesse had more
hotels, but Suzann had Boardwalk and Park Place. It was
Jesse's turn. He didn't reach for the dice.

"When I got back to the lake, you had already left," he said.

"You came back?" asked Suzann.

"Yeah, I came back to the lake."

"Why?"

"I didn't want you to think I was deserting you."

"You aren't deserting me?"

Jesse didn't answer immediately and she knew her fears hadn't been without foundation. Finally he said, "Suzann, I think you're wonderful."

Now her suspicions were confirmed. "If I'm so wonderful, why are you about to tell me good-bye?"

"If I had met you first, maybe it would have been different," he said.

This was obviously hard for him. His voice was strained, and he was having difficulty meeting her gaze. She could make it easier on him. But his position held the advantage in the long run, and this hadn't exactly been her lucky day, either.

"Different than what?" she asked.

"Different than me sitting here having to tell you something that I wish I didn't have to say." Jesse looked down. His fingers were straightening a row of houses on Marvin Gardens. "You almost made me forget Carolyn. But tonight, being with her again was like ripping open a wound that hadn't healed. I'm sorry. Really. I hate myself for doing this to you."

She'd make it easier. "It's okay. Anyway, you taught me something very important."

Jesse's face showed curiosity but he didn't question her.

"I don't have to have someone," she continued. "You've taught me I don't have to have someone. Do you know what that means?'

"I'm not sure. It wasn't exactly my intention."

"But it was an important thing for me to learn. When Ann told me you had left the lake with Carolyn, I knew. I knew my turn was over. Do you believe clairvoyant tendencies can develop later in life?"

Jesse shook his head in a noncommittal way.

"Then, slowly, through the disappointment, through the pain, it came to me. Even alone, even by myself, I'm okay. My

128

life's going to be okay. I'll miss you, Jesse, but I'll be okay."
Just to talk like that was making her feel strong. The determination reflected in her face, enhancing the natural beauty of her features with a radiant vitality.

"You're amazing. Really. I know I'm giving up a great deal. But you'll find someone wonderful. I know you will."

"Jesse, I meant it about not having to have someone else. For a long time I thought I couldn't live without Peter, and then without you. But I can live. I can live a rich life. The quality of it depends only on me."

"I see what you mean, Suzann. I'm glad you feel that way. But sometimes it's when you stop needing something that it drops into your lap."

# 16

The Rose who welcomed her staff to the Sunday morning presidency meeting was not the same. Not only had a new determination to renovate her appearance been kindled on the inside, but the change had already been manifested on the outside as well. Twenty hours earlier, Rose had watched as Peggy of New Image Hair Designs had cut and permed the long, limp hairstyle which had carried Rose through the past decade.

"I love it!" exclaimed Carolyn. She sat down in Rose's rocker as the clock was chiming four out of nine. "It really looks nice on you."

Rose, an awkward receptor of compliments, changed the subject quickly. "How's Tyler doing? I checked on him before I went home Friday night, but he was sleeping."

"He's moving a little slow, but he'll be okay."

Suzann and Elaine arrived and added their praise for Rose's new look.

"I was thinking about getting my hair cut that way, too," said Elaine.

"You should. They have some good magazine articles out this month to read while you're waiting," answered Rose, anxious to take the focus off her hair. "Shall we get started?"

After a prayer and the previous week's minutes, they discussed the Pursuit of Excellence program and a sister who would need some compassionate service this month. Then

Rose launched into the September ward activity. "It's going to be at the park across from the church. We aren't having a dinner, just homemade ice cream and cake. The elders said— if you can believe this—they'd do the cakes if we make the ice cream. Bill Reardon is in charge of the food. For those who are interested, they'll have some coed softball, too. Jesse Mitchell is in charge of that." Rose looked up to see if his name would cause a sensation. Suzann and Carolyn were engrossed in their notebooks; only she and Elaine exchanged glances.

Rose continued, "They want to offer an alternate activity for those Forty-ninth Warders who will purposely forget their mitts. Anyone have any ideas?"

"There will be mostly girls," said Carolyn. "They could make a quilt."

"Or go to a movie," offered Suzann.

Rose was relieved. Presidency meeting was back to normal. It was as if she hadn't even mentioned Jesse's name; it was like it used to be before he had started agitating their lives.

"What I had in mind was along the line of Bingo," said Rose. "We could offer prizes, just a little something to make it exciting . . . like a trip to Hawaii . . ."

They agreed on Bingo. They agreed on the trip to Hawaii, too, but Rose warned them she'd have trouble pushing it through.

"Suzann, homemaking night is Thursday. Are the mini-classes all set?"

"All set." Suzann turned to Carolyn. "You might even find some useful after all."

"I didn't mean to get on you about your wedding-oriented mini-classes . . ." Carolyn began. And then she stopped. "Why did you say that?"

"Because I expect to hear an announcement. Unless you're going to turn Jesse down a second time. . . ."

"Suzann, I don't know what you mean. After we took Tyler to the hospital, Jesse went back to the lake. He went back to you."

"He didn't come back to me. He never got over you. He just came back to break the news."

"How do you know? What did he say?"

"Would it be possible to postpone this discussion until after the meeting?" Rose interrupted meekly. "I know Jesse was on the agenda this time, but that was actually just regarding softball."

"Oh, sure," answered Carolyn, fully aware that she'd be thinking of nothing else until the subject was resumed.

The excerpts from Suzann's Friday night conversation with Jesse were worth waiting for. Carolyn listened intently as a trickle of promise seeped into her heart. But it was just as the words were becoming deliciously sweet that Carolyn's conscience woke up.

"I'm sorry. This must be hard for you," she told Suzann. "And you're being so nice to me."

"You were nice to me."

"Before or after I apologized about the mini-classes?"

"I don't even remember that you suggested having a mini-class to catch a man." There was teasing in Suzann's voice, but no rancor.

"Maybe Rose said it." Carolyn smiled, but the smile slipped from her lips and it was a face marked by pain, not joy that repeated, "I'm sorry, Suzann."

"I know." Suzann smiled. The stalwart. She was going to make it through this. There had been moments of anguish, and there would be more. But she opened her own doors now. She could get through.

Rose often offered a snack after the closing prayer, and this morning she passed a tray of vegetables. "I'm afraid you'll be seeing fewer cinnamon rolls and blueberry muffins and more carrot and celery sticks for a while."

"Can I be released?" Suzann joked.

"I don't know if this diet of yours is such a good idea," added Elaine.

But Carolyn quietly took a carrot and headed for the door. She had inedible things on her mind.

*Maybe I should have stayed by the phone yesterday,* thought Carolyn. *Between checking out Tyler and picking up Alice and going for Chinese food, I was gone most of the day. I could have missed Jesse's call. But Mom was home. She*

132

*would have notified me red alert if Jesse had phoned. Maybe he didn't call. Maybe he's not going to call. Maybe he expects me to make the first move; he thinks I should come to him because it was my stubbornness which severed our relationship. But I already blurted out that I loved him. What more could he want? I'll just wait. He'll call sooner or later. Now that I know he cares about me, I can be patient.*

Carolyn saw Jesse a few times at church. In Sunday School, he sat across the room, separated by a sea of Forty-ninth Warders. They exchanged glances too fleeting to reveal emotion. Carolyn almost approached Jesse after class, but when she saw him talking with another girl, she turned away.

Walking home from her meetings, Carolyn considered altering her plans. *Maybe patience is an overrated virtue,* she decided. *There's nothing wrong with making the first move.*

Carolyn had been to Jesse's office—that cool oasis off Dobson Road—several times, but only once with an appointment. Although Jesse's secretary acknowledged her with a smile, Carolyn wasn't sure if she remembered her name and wondered whether she should identify herself. But the secretary buzzed Jesse, so Carolyn assumed she had been announced.

"He'd like you to go on back," said the secretary.

Carolyn was studying a new painting that had joined his collection since their separation. She lingered beside it just a moment before walking the short hallway to Jesse's office.

Jesse gazed at Carolyn for several minutes. His eyes smiled, but his manner remained businesslike. "Sit down. Let me guess; you're writing a paper on how computers have changed in the past five years?"

"Not even close. I have a real problem. In September we're having a coed softball game and I don't know the proper way to hold the bat. I'm afraid I'll be the laughingstock of the whole ward."

Jesse regarded her sly grin before replying, "Would you like to talk about it over lunch?"

"I'd rather just have lunch."

"The usual place?"

"Of course."

For the past couple of months, Carolyn had avoided the restaurant decorated with colorful tile and swirling wrought-iron work that had the best Mexican food in the country and was practically within walking distance of Jesse's office. Only because they arrived at 11:30, slightly before the regular lunch hour, were they seated immediately.

"Do you want to see a menu?" asked Jesse, even though Carolyn had an unbroken record for ordering flautas.

"Yes. I want the one with the marriage proposal." After she had said it, Carolyn regretted being so bold.

If her reply caught Jesse off guard, he didn't show it. He just gave her a scrutinizing look and said, "Before I hand you another customized menu, I want to be sure you're not still the needle in the haystack."

"The needle?"

"The only girl in the Forty-ninth Ward who doesn't want to get married."

"I've changed." How could she explain? She borrowed a concept from one of her recent research papers. "When you're deciding about something, you have to be open to fresh impressions, and as you reassess the situation, if the balance starts to tip the other way, you can't be afraid to change your mind."

"What tipped the balance?"

"I missed you. I decided while writing is always going to be a major part of my life, it will never be more important than you."

"What about a family?"

"I could have a family and still write. Maybe I'd have to cut down my projected words per day, because there has to be time to listen and read and cuddle and probably even wash hair. There's so much for a child to learn, and you never know how long that child will be with you. . . ."

Carolyn's explanation was followed by a measure of silence.

"And now I'm supposed to propose again?" Jesse asked. He said it softly, but Carolyn couldn't tell if there was a trace of sarcasm to his question.

"Only if you still want me to marry you."

"It's going to take three days to get another menu printed up."

"Some people get engaged without menus."

Jesse took Carolyn's hands across the table. At first he held them tightly, but then he loosened his grip until he was gently massaging them in his own. "Are you sure you want to get married?"

"I accept."

Jesse smiled. "Why do I feel like you're always one step ahead of me? It makes me wonder if I'm going to be able to handle you. . . . And yet, somehow, I think that's why I love you."

The waitress rustled her pad to capture their attention. "Excuse me. Are you ready?"

"Absolutely," answered Carolyn.